Praise for *Legacy of Learning*

A wholehearted, insightful delight to read! In this deeply human and relatable book, Meghan Lawson gives us tools and strategies to continuously improve and create genuine moments that are profoundly positive for ourselves and for those we serve. If you are looking for small moves that make a big impact and create a legacy of empowered learning and living, this is the book for you!
—**Lainie Rowell, bestselling author, award-winning educator, and TEDx speaker**

Legacy of Learning is a shot in the arm for anyone working in a school: deeply insightful, dead-on practical, and undeniably stirring. An education lifer, Lawson knows how relentlessly challenging it is to work in school, and she knows how to find—and mine—the silver linings. Get this book for any teacher or school leader you know who needs to be reminded of how big of a deal they are.
—**Mike Kleba, high school teacher, cohost of the NYEdTech Meetup, and author of *Otherful: How to Change the World (and Your School) through Other People***

For years, I have connected with Meghan Lawson on social media and followed her inspiring blog. When I would read one of her blog posts, I would say to myself, "I sure hope Meghan writes a book soon." The waiting has paid off, and we now have an engaging masterpiece in our hands for book talks, reflections, and doable application. *Legacy of Learning* is a work that I will revisit many times. This is a book that takes on one of the most unexplored and important aspects of our profession as educators: legacy. Meghan Lawson writes with such a sincere and empathetic voice. Her words invite all on a journey to connect our educational dots to a tapestry of the legacy we leave behind to impact others. Reading this book is an invitation to embrace our beautiful humanity and tap into the positive impact we can have on our school communities.
—**Sean Gaillard, principal, podcaster, author of *The Pepper Effect***

Relevant, empowering, and insightful. Woven throughout *Legacy of Learning* are touching and deeply personal stories that guide us through how to take small actions that make a lasting impact on our mindset as we work toward embracing and enjoying what our daily lives have to offer. This inspirational book is great for anyone who is looking for practical tips to improve your overall well-being and effectiveness as an educator. Highly recommend!

—**Livia Chan, head teacher, author, and presenter**

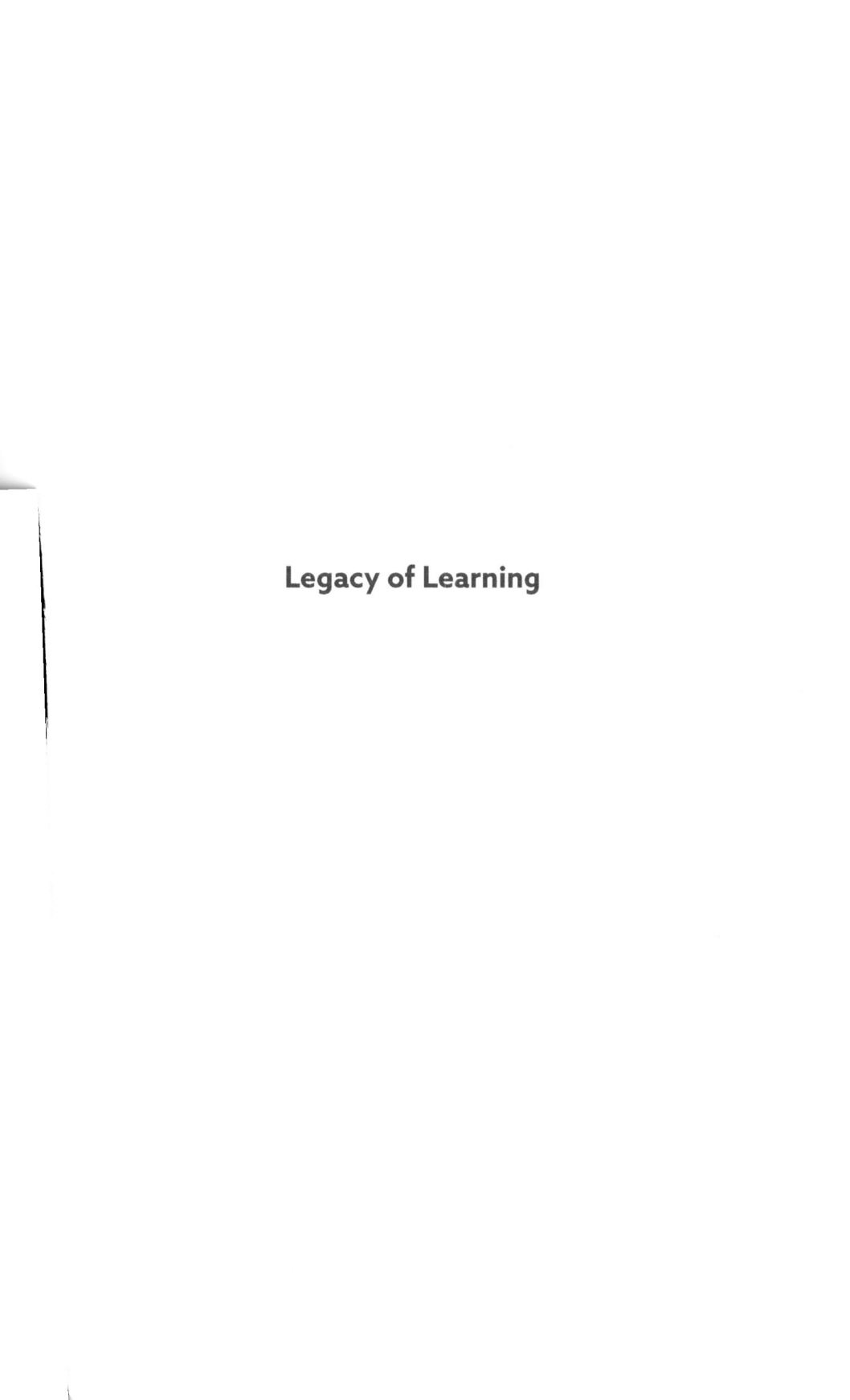

Legacy of Learning

LEGACY OF LEARNING
Teaching for Lasting Impact

Meghan Lawson

Legacy of Learning: Teaching for Lasting Impact
© 2023 Meghan Lawson

All rights reserved. No part of this publication may be reproduced in any form or by any electronic or mechanical means, including information storage and retrieval systems, without permission in writing by the publisher, except by a reviewer who may quote brief passages in a review. For information regarding permission, contact the publisher at books@impressbooks.org.

> This book is available at special discounts when purchased in quantity for educational purposes or for use as premiums, promotions, or fundraisers. For inquiries and details, contact the publisher at books@impressbooks.org.

Published by IMPress, a division of Dave Burgess Consulting, Inc.
IMPressbooks.org
DaveBurgessConsulting.com
San Diego, CA

Paperback ISBN: 978-1-948334-68-6
Ebook ISBN: 978-1-948334-69-3

Cover and interior designed by Liz Schreiter
Edited and produced by Reading List Editorial
ReadingListEditorial.com

IM

To the people in my life who make me feel calm and capable.

CONTENTS

Introduction 1
Chapter 1: Happiness Is Celebrating Growth 7
Chapter 2: We Are Not Pizza. 22
Chapter 3: Ridiculously in Charge 42
Chapter 4: Mosquito Moves 53
Chapter 5: Nourish the Blooms 62
Chapter 6: Popsicles and Conga Lines. 82
Chapter 7: Wholehearted Work 107
Conclusion 120
Notes. 123
Acknowledgments. 129
About Meghan Lawson 130
More from IMPress 131

INTRODUCTION

Each educator's journey began in a different place. Some of us played school at home growing up. Some of us grew up with parents who were educators. Some of us had difficult school experiences, and we wanted to become teachers so we could reinvent what school could be.

In my case, I didn't want to be a teacher. I wanted to be a Broadway dancer, and I wanted to study dance in college. My mom, Kim Lawson, a single parent, was very practical and understood that I did not need a degree in dance to become a professional dancer. She also knew it was difficult to make it on Broadway. So, she insisted that I earn a degree in a different field as my backup plan.

Very quickly, my backup plan became my actual plan. I didn't love teaching at the start. You read that right. I learned through student teaching in a high school ELA classroom that this was going to be a lot of work. I learned that there was no applause for thoughtful lesson plans. I learned that grading papers took a lot of time outside of the school day and that early mornings came back around fast. I learned to drink my coffee black.

I learned a lot of things in my early years of teaching. But perhaps the most important lesson I learned was that this work matters. In a big way. And something about that has kept me coming back. It's what keeps a lot of us coming back. It feels good to do work that matters so deeply. It feels good to matter in the lives of so many.

And while I can finally say that I love our profession, there are times when I question whether it's all worth it. It seems like the work continues to become more complex, challenging, and exhausting.

There are national shortages of educators. Many of my colleagues are telling their own children not to become teachers. Think about that. It's so difficult and at times the conditions are so miserable that actual educators are keeping their own kids from becoming teachers because they want better for them. I want better for all of us too. There is a lot of work to be done on the systems of school to make school a place where adults want to work every day and where kids want to learn.

And in the meantime, that leaves us where? It leaves us trying to control what we can control. It leaves us trying to figure out how to do our personal best. It leaves us trying to figure out how to stay encouraged so we keep showing up for our students who desperately need us. For a world that so desperately needs us.

Whenever I think about quitting, I think of Mrs. Boggess, my first-grade teacher. I needed her more than I've ever needed a teacher. Because on February 12, 1989, my dad lost his battle with leukemia. I can remember the day my mom came home from the hospital to tell us. She sat on my canopy bed and tried to find the words. My dad and I were very close. It was difficult to comprehend this terrible loss. I flew off my bed and ran to the window, where in a fit of grief, hot tears running down my face, I managed to rip the blinds off. While my body was out of control with this grief, my mind suddenly became clear. I turned to my mom, looked her square in the eyes, and asked, "Will we have enough food to eat?" During those formative years of my life, my mom had stayed home to raise us. I understood that my dad went to work to provide for us. Now that he was gone, I wondered how we would survive without him.

When it was time for me to go back to school, it was hard to imagine letting my mom out of my sight. I can still remember her pulling the car up in front of my elementary school. I remember the heaviness in my body. I can remember the fear I felt. It was going to take herculean strength to pull that door handle and walk out the door away from her. Until I saw them. My classmates. They were standing

Introduction

at the front door with their faces pressed against the glass, waving and cheering for me to come into the school.

It was as if Mrs. Boggess knew exactly what I needed at that moment and had rolled out the red carpet for my arrival. She could have tried to play it cool and make it normal, but she knew this wasn't normal and that I needed some encouragement. This was a bold move that turned out to be the right move. And for the rest of that school year, she had my back. Over and over again. There were times when I needed a lot of grace, which she gave to me. She was exactly what I needed during that difficult time.

I'm so glad Mrs. Boggess showed up. I'm so glad she didn't quit. I still get emotional thinking about the impact she had on me. That's legacy work right there. I reached out to Mrs. Boggess while writing this book. I was surprised to learn that she lived in the neighborhood where I grew up. The same neighborhood I lived in when she was my first-grade teacher. I took my time to carefully write my words on a card to explain just how much she meant to me. Imagine my joy when a couple of weeks later, she replied. Her card was filled with artfully written cursive letters and her adult account of our time together. She wrote:

> Hi Meghan,
>
> I'm so sorry it has taken me so long to respond to your lovely note. My mail was stopped as my husband and I were on a cruise. Brandy (my daughter) told me that you had written me. I'm honored that you have included me in your upcoming book. How special is that?
>
> I remember you and your 1st grade year very well. You had been telling me for quite a while that your daddy would be coming home from the hospital on Valentine's Day. If memory serves me correctly, he passed away either on or near Valentine's Day. My heart broke for you. I attended his funeral. How sad. He was so young. I thought

how are we going to help this sweet little girl get through this. The only thing I knew to do was make your classroom a safe, caring, loving place to come to each day. The other children (even at 6 years old) understood what we needed to do to take care of you and make school a happy place for you to be. It warms my heart to hear from you that we handled it in the right way.

I remember seeing your dance competitions a few years later as Brandy danced too. You were a talented little dancer, and I was so proud of you. As for our neighborhood, we have lived in the same house for over 50 years. I knew that you lived in [the same neighborhood] when you were in my class. You were too young to realize it.

It is wonderful to see that you are happy in your personal and professional life.

Hearing from former students and a note like yours makes my thirty years of teaching worthwhile.

Love always,
Linda Boggess
PS: Let me know when your book comes out. ☺

I was amazed by the details she remembered, and it was powerful to hear the perspective of an adult who knew me during such a difficult time in my childhood.

I noticed in her response that she mentioned not being sure what to do at first. Such a relatable feeling as an educator. We are often unsure if we are making the right decisions. When she decided that the only thing she knew to do was to make the classroom a "safe, caring, loving place to come to each day," it was the exact thing I needed most. I'm so grateful she followed her "teacher gut" and encouraged my classmates to join her in supporting me. We have instincts as educators. Sometimes, we question those instincts because there are many

Introduction

voices telling us what we should do. Often, the feeling comes to us in a whisper, but it almost always sends us in the right direction if we can tune into it. Mrs. Boggess's letter was a kind reminder to trust our gut. Additionally, she trusted the class to make the classroom a happy place for me, and I felt that from them. We are never too young to make a difference. Our students can make a positive difference in our classrooms and schools today. Finally, she shared the credit. She explained, "It warms my heart to hear from you that we handled it in the right way." Whether we are growing a positive culture in the classroom, a school, or a district, sharing the credit is an effective strategy for cultivating a sense of belonging and ownership. In a short letter, Mrs. Boggess managed to give a master class in classroom culture. It doesn't have to be complicated to be impactful.

You have deeply impacted students too. Some of them will tell you about your impact and many may never tell you, but you are leaving a legacy. You are giving others the strength to move forward, the strength to believe in themselves, the strength to try to make this world a better place. Knowing this makes being an educator so meaningful.

But we don't have to suffer while we make this kind of impact. In fact, the more we can live well and be well, the more our impact will grow. When we can discern what really matters to us and what matters less, we can give more energy in the places that matter most. When we are clear about what matters most for learners, we are more likely to inspire the best in our students and colleagues.

Inside each of us is the educator and human being we always wanted to be. I hope this book helps you find your way forward. Because this world needs you now more than ever. With some small moves and intentionality, you can live a really good life while making a lasting impact on learners.

As an aside, I had a difficult time with the title for this book, as many of those closest to me can attest. During a conversation with George Couros, we uncovered that my struggle came from my immense care for educators and my overwhelming appreciation for their work, which matters so deeply. Educators spend much of their lives nurturing the hearts and minds of learners. They deserve to have their hearts and minds nourished too. I hope this book is affirming, energizing, and thought provoking—because the legacy of educators lives on in each of us, past, present, and future. Thank you for picking up this book and for all you do to support the growth and development of others.

CHAPTER 1

HAPPINESS IS CELEBRATING GROWTH

I did then what I knew how to do. Now that I know better, I do better.

—MAYA ANGELOU

Happy educators lead happy schools. Happiness is a personal practice and not always an easy one. Depending on the number of obstacles we face, experiencing meaningful levels of happiness may be more or less accessible. Certainly, there are many factors at play, and not all of our happiness is contingent upon our choices and mindset alone. But it's a worthy cause. We deserve the opportunity to be happier.

Shawn Achor is a happiness researcher from Harvard and a *New York Times* best-selling author. Much of his work is centered on the connection between happiness and success. In his TED talk, "The Happy Secret to Better Work," Achor posits that "your brain at positive is 31 percent more productive than your brain at negative, neutral, or stressed."[1] Thirty-one percent. Think about how significant 31 percent could be. Imagine if you had 31 percent more time, 31 percent more money, 31 percent more sleep. Thirty-one percent is no joke. Yet we don't spend much time explicitly talking about happiness and the role it plays in our performance and productivity. Dopamine is a chemical neurotransmitter that is released in the brain when we have positive feelings. According to Achor, "Dopamine, which floods into your system when you're positive, has two functions. Not only does it make you happier, it turns on all of the learning centers of the brain."[2] When we pursue our own happiness, we improve our ability to think deeply about the learners we serve and we improve our ability to respond effectively to their needs.

From Goal Setting to Goal Growth Celebrations

A simple synonym for *happiness* is *growth*. It might seem like a stretch, but can you think of a time when you recognized your own growth and didn't experience positive emotions? The process of growing can be painful at times. But when we give ourselves space and the opportunity to acknowledge that we are not in the place we once were, this can lead to happiness. J. B. Yeats described it this way: "And happiness . . . what is it? I say it is neither virtue nor pleasure nor this thing or that, but simply *growth*. We are happy when we are growing."[3]

Our happiness levels as educators matter in a big way because our growth matters in a big way. Training our minds to see and celebrate growth in ourselves and other people is critical to growing happiness in ourselves and others. This is not to say that we should suspend positive emotions until we can see growth. It is quite the opposite. By enjoying the process of working toward our goals, we increase the likelihood that we'll do great work. Growing teachers lead growth-filled classrooms, which leads to higher happiness levels for everyone. While happiness alone is difficult to measure, we can approach our work with learners in ways that uplift and inspire. We can start by creating space for individuals to recognize their progress toward goals.

As a middle school English teacher, I placed significant emphasis on goal setting in my classroom. First, I had students write our state standards in developmentally appropriate language. An example of a goal would be "I can determine central ideas or themes and provide a summary or thorough analysis of the text." After breaking this goal into smaller learning targets and providing instruction, I would assess their understanding. Students would read a short text they had never seen and then identify the central idea and explain their reasoning. To gauge their true understanding, it was important to ensure I didn't use a text we were working with as a class. These were not assessments to discern whether students had been listening in class. Rather, these were assessments of their understanding of theme and their ability to both identify it in a text and explain it soundly. After grading the assessments, I would have students take a colored pencil and shade in an empty bar graph indicating their level of progress toward the goal. For example, if a student mastered identifying a central idea or theme but was still struggling to provide an accurate summary or sound analysis, they would shade their progress toward the goal halfway. When students had not yet mastered a particular learning target, I would organize them in small groups to facilitate further learning and then reassess them with a different text they had never seen. If they made progress, students would add additional shading on their bar graph for the corresponding learning target. I was proud that we were setting goals in my class because clear learning expectations are important. We can't hit a target we can't see. However, what I failed to realize at the time was how important it was for students to celebrate their own growth on the path to mastery. We acknowledged it, but I didn't make a big deal of it. That was a missed opportunity. That was where the emphasis needed to be—on the growth rather than the distance to the final destination.

As Rita Pierson says in her TED talk, "Every Kid Needs a Champion," "I gave a quiz, twenty questions. A student missed

GROWTH CELEBRATIONS

eighteen. I put a plus two on his paper and a big smiley face. He said, 'Ms. Pierson, is this an F?' I said, 'Yes.' He said, 'Then, why'd you put a smiley face?' I said, 'Because you're on a roll. You got two right. You didn't miss them all.' I said, 'And when we review this, won't you do better?' He said, 'Yes, ma'am. I can do better.' You see—eighteen sucks all the life out of you. Plus two said, 'I ain't all bad.'"[4] You see, it's not "This is where you need to be" that inspires. Rather, it's "Look at how far you've come!"

We can learn a good deal from this bar graph example. As Shawn Achor explains in his TED talk, "If we can find a way to be more positive in the present, then our brains work more successfully."[5] The brain is more motivated by what we have achieved than by how far we have to go. I can be guilty of putting off happiness by putting off recognizing my own growth. For example, I work out with a personal trainer every week. For the first couple of years, I was solely focused on a number I wanted to see on the scale and on certain aspects of my physique. But my personal trainer, Wendell Whitehead Jr., has taken videos of me working out from the very beginning. He will go back through videos or his notes and point out how much I've increased my strength. Every time he does this, it's inspiring to see how far I've come. That makes me happy and makes me want to work harder; it makes me want to be more disciplined in ways that looking at a long-term goal never could. In fact, I'm much less inclined to weigh myself now or obsess over my personal physique aspirations. I'm focused on getting stronger and feeling confident in my clothes. I'm happily focused on how far I've come rather than how far I have to go.

Tracking can be a great way to see progress over time. This is why so many of us are drawn to counting steps and those water bottles that tell us how much water we drank today. But it's critical to consider our tracking data in growth-inspiring ways. Every ounce of water we drink is more water than we started with that day. Every step we take is one more step than we had at the start of the day. Sometimes, we can look back and see that we have taken more steps or consumed more water than we did a week ago or month ago, but if we can't see that kind of progress, then what? Well, it's important to be thoughtful about how we speak to ourselves. Recently, I had a health scare, and I was dealing with some emotionally and mentally taxing stressors that were not part of my life a couple of months prior. So, my progress toward some of my goals did not look the same. But if you have 50 percent to give, and you give 50 percent, then you gave 100 percent. Forward is forward, and it's vital that you take good care of how you think about yourself and the progress you're making. No matter how small. You're trying, and you're making progress.

As educators, it's easy to become discouraged by everything we are not doing. If we don't train our minds to see what we are doing well and what's going well, then it's hard to see anything other than what's not going right. Many of us spend our time thinking we should be doing this and we should be doing that. But our growth does not come from a place of *should*. Our growth comes from a place of *can*. It's not just our ability to perform at a higher level—it's our ability to maintain our current level of success. Look at what I *can* do. Look at what I did. Look at what I am doing right now. Especially that last one. Look at what I am doing right now.

For too long, I was so focused getting better that I missed the opportunity to be proud of myself for continuing the path. If I can do ten push-ups, and it remains true that I can do ten push-ups a year from now, this means I have maintained my strength. Maintaining means we aren't going backward. We might not be where we want to be, and we will likely adjust our plan to increase our strength, but maintaining is something to be celebrated too. If I experience an injury and manage to get back to eight consecutive push-ups after a long recovery year, that is progress. Those are eight push-ups that I could not do at the start of my injury. Training our mind to see the growth and good in the moment is a wonderful strategy for enjoyment. Enjoying the moment gives us freedom from worries about the past or anxiety about the future. Choosing to focus on what we can do and choosing to be happy in the moment are great ways to shape the future because our perception is our reality. If we perceive that we are having a positive impact on ourselves and the world around us, our confidence that we can and will do good work in the future grows. In a *Forbes* article by Dan Schawbel titled "What You Need to Do Before Experiencing Happiness," Shawn Achor explains, "What your brain attends to becomes your reality. Based on this research, the best way to change your reality is to first realize that there are multiple realities from which you could choose. I could focus on the one failure in front of me, or spend my brain's resources processing the two new doors of opportunity that have opened. One reality leads to paralysis, the other to positive change."[6]

Positive change through learning and experiences is what education is all about. If we, as educators, can change the way we see ourselves and see our own capability and potential, we can also change how students perceive themselves and their potential.

Emotional Contagion

So how does our individual happiness spread to those around us? Some attribute it to mirror neurons, though some scientists now disagree.[7] I don't claim to be an expert or to fully understand why, but it does appear that there are times when we mimic the emotions of others without even thinking about it. This means that emotions are potentially contagious. And if emotions can be contagious, it's vital to spread the good stuff because students may catch our feelings. This means that if educators enter school excited about the day and offer a big smile, friendly conversation, and concern for others, kids will catch on. They start to feel excited about that day. They start to feel friendly. They start to feel more care for others.

I experienced this as an elementary principal. When I would stand in the front of the school, I would greet students with special handshakes, high fives, hugs, and smiles. It was clear that some students were bringing heavy hearts to school. I also watched some students try *not* to smile at me. They tried to be cool, calm, collected, but more often than not, I would see that smile they were fighting back start to creep in. My ability to elicit more smiles felt like growth. Students grew into positive attitudes, and I grew in my ability to impact them in a positive way.

Now, don't get me wrong, the goal isn't to "make people happy." Forcing emotions onto others doesn't feel right or good. The goal is to simply give people greater access to higher happiness levels and their greatest potential. Many of our students and staff are carrying around heavy emotions and experiences. They don't owe us a smile or a faked reaction to our attempts at connection. But what we owe them is to see them and love them in whatever emotion or state they show up in daily. That's another reason why I loved greeting kids at the start of the school day. Even if they did show up feeling low, my hope was that access to happy adults could offer them even the slightest positive impact. Every little bit counts.

Authentic, Positive Feedback

An unexpected way to bring more happiness to students is through specific, authentic, positive feedback. One of my favorite strategies for sharing positive feedback comes from Mike Rutherford, author of *The Artisan Teacher*. It's called "30 Second Feedback" because it's intended to take only thirty seconds. It's a great way to evoke growth in a strengths-focused way. This strategy is focused on feedback for teachers, but I believe it could work with students as well. Often, when we hear about growth-evoking feedback, we think that means a deficit is being addressed. However, this feedback is about pointing out something that is going really well. Again, pointing out what's going well is inspiring because it helps us see our potential. When we can see our potential to do good things, that makes us want to accelerate our growth.

People need to hear what they are doing well—shared with great specificity so they believe it. They need to hear this over and over. In fact, in the Gallup Q^{12} survey, which measures employee engagement, there is the following item: "In the last seven days, I have received recognition or praise for doing good work." Gallup's explanation for this item asserts that "employees who do not feel adequately recognized are twice as likely to say they'll quit in the next year."[8] Adults and kids alike want to be recognized for their hard work and contributions. We also want to be recognized in the ways that work best for us as individuals. We spend so much time focused on whether people know their areas of perceived deficit. Without positive feedback, meaningful relationships, and proximity, hard truths feel extra harsh. So, we must be intentional and consistent with our positive feedback. For example, it does not take long to write a little something on a Post-it. This small move, when leveraged consistently over time, can have a tremendous impact on energy and effort.

Here is my own example of Mike Rutherford's strategy.[9] Let's say you go into a classroom and see the class seated on the rug while the teacher delivers a mini-lesson. Move closer so you can see and hear them accurately, and take the time to be present and really notice staff and student actions and interactions. Then, write the teacher a note. It might sound something like:

> Thank you so much for having me! When you paused your mini-lesson and asked students to turn and talk, it gave them the opportunity to share what they were thinking, and when students share what they are thinking, they often think more deeply. Nice move!

Let's deconstruct that a bit so you can consider how you might use this strategy with staff (or modify it to use with students).[10]

CUSHION: Thank you so much for having me!

TEACHING & LEARNING: When you asked students to turn and talk (**teaching**), it gave them the opportunity to share what they were thinking, and when students share what they are thinking, they often think more deeply (**learning**).

+ TAG: Nice move!

30 SECOND FEEDBACK

Cushion → **Teaching** → **Learning** → **+Tag**

Cushion	Teaching	Learning	+Tag
A courtesy statement such as "I enjoyed being in your classroom today…" or "Thanks for having me in for a few moments."	Specifically identify a moment of teaching such as "When you knelt down and worked with Laura to correct her paper…" or "When you held the globe in your hand.."	Specifically identify one positive learning effect that followed from the specific episode of teaching. For example, "She focused and gave extra effort in response to your attention" or "Everyone's eyes were on you anticipating what you might do next."	An upbeat finish/ compliment such as "That really worked" or "That was an effective way to deal with the situation" or "Nice move!"

We can use strategies such as thirty-second feedback to inspire growth—and spark happiness—in our students and our colleagues, but we can also inspire growth in ourselves. There is no professional growth without self-work, and there is no happiness without growth. The most important work we do is the work we do on ourselves. Everything else is secondary.

The Cognitive Triangle

When the work feels hard, and let's be real, it feels hard every day, the best way to change our perception of the situation is to change our perception of ourselves in the situation. Our ability to change our thoughts is the biggest and most impactful growth move of all. I recently learned about the cognitive triangle, a concept that's rooted in cognitive behavioral therapy. It was developed by Dr. Aaron Beck, researcher and Emeritus professor of psychiatry at the University of

Pennsylvania in the 1960s,[11] and goes something like this: Our thoughts impact our feelings and our feelings impact our behavior. So, if we can change our thoughts, then we can change our feelings and ultimately change our behavior.

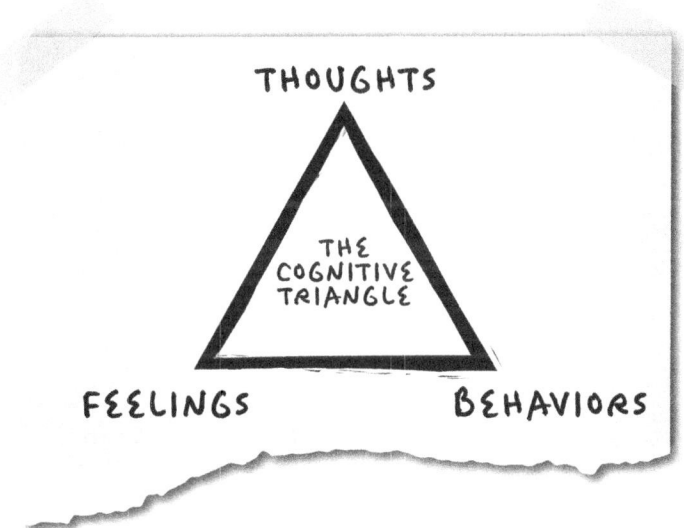

Real growth isn't always measured by the number of push-ups we can do, our performance on an evaluation, or the number of tasks we check off our to-do lists. Sometimes, personal growth can be measured by how we respond to what's happening around us—and our ability to change our thoughts to positively impact our feelings.

For example, a teacher recently told me how much she missed seeing me. You may interpret that as a small, kind, innocent comment intended to make me feel seen and cared for, but that is not how I received it. One of my personal values is proximity. As a director of secondary teaching and learning, I make a point to spend most of my time in the school buildings. I make sure that I walk the hallways of our middle school and say hi to people. I ensure that I don't cut corners. I even walk to the end of the dead-end hallways. Depending on the time of day and what's happening in lessons, doors may be closed or teachers may be out of their rooms, but I smile and wave to whomever I can. I mark time off on my calendar to ensure this gets done because it's a big priority for me. Hearing that comment made me feel like I was not living out my values, like my efforts had been worthless—all from that one seemingly innocuous comment.

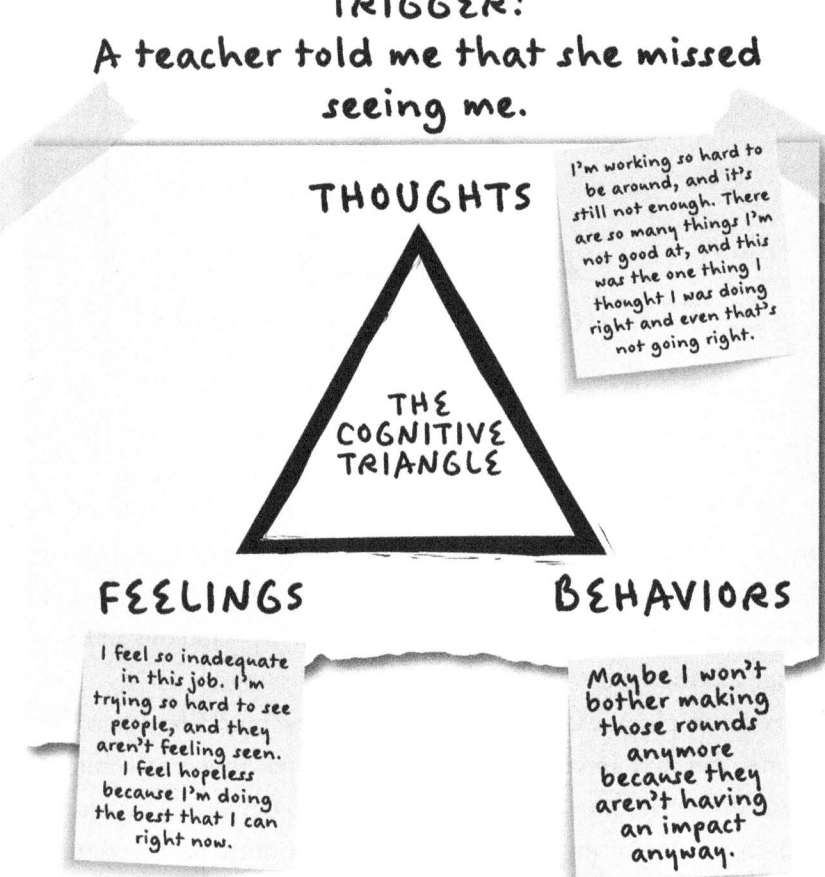

Luckily, my thoughts didn't play out like that for too long. The great thing about the cognitive triangle is that it clearly illustrates how thoughts inflect feelings and behaviors. So I realized I needed a replacement thought.

Happiness Is Celebrating Growth

Now, I've not mastered this. I continue to learn the same lessons over and over again. I continue to struggle with the same patterns of thinking. However, more often than not, I now catch it when it's happening. These days, when a staff member tells me they miss me, I replace my initial thought with more productive thoughts. In doing so, I change how I feel and how I respond to how I feel. It takes practice, and progress isn't linear. Sometimes I will slip back into my old thinking. This often happens when I'm tired and coping with other stress.

Growth isn't a steady incline. Growth is a steady study of ourselves. When I find myself back in old patterns of thinking, I ask myself,

"Where do I think this is coming from?" Then I try reframing my thinking to see how that impacts my feelings and reactions.

It needs to be said that space to feel our feelings is important. It also needs to be said that some situations are simply bad and bad for us. If we are being abused or mistreated or see the same happening to others, the focus is not on changing our thoughts and feelings. The focus is on safety. The cognitive triangle is intended for safe situations in which we are experiencing unproductive thoughts.

Our Reptilian Brains

Unproductive thoughts often run rampant through our psyche. We come by it honestly because our brains are wired to look for threats to our safety. Dr. Laurel Mellin explains this in her book *Wired for Joy*: "The most primitive area of the brain is the smallest, the oldest, and the quickest. Sitting at the base of the skull, it is quite similar to the entire brain of a reptile. It determines your alertness and is the home base of the fight or flight response. The reptile brain or the brain stem reacts very quickly so that if a lion is chasing you, you don't sit around wondering what kind of lion it is or share a few choice words with it. You escape. The trouble with the reptilian brain is that because there aren't lions roaming into your village these days, it is often a loose cannon, firing but not very accurately."[12]

So, unfortunately, our brain struggles to identify the difference between a threat to safety and a threat to ego. That is what causes misfires in thinking. That's why I struggled with that little comment from the teacher who missed seeing me. I received it as a threat to my ego. The good news is that the brain is coachable. We can retrain our brain into patterns of thinking that better serve us. Our students can do it too. Remember, thoughts lead to feelings and feelings lead to behavior. And wow, when we do that, when we practice new ways of thinking, the new ways of thinking start to get easier. When those new ways of thinking start to feel natural and habitual, that's incredible growth. How gratifying! The only thing we can control at the end of the day is ourselves. Making positive changes in the way we show up every day is empowering, uplifting, and possibly contagious.

It can be contagious because students and colleagues are watching us. If we continue to look harshly upon ourselves and our potential in front of others, it makes them question themselves. Especially when they look up to us—and often our students do. If we speak about our mistakes in ways that sound like we are stuck and can never change, it places doubt in the minds of those around us about their potential too.

We must talk to ourselves and about ourselves thoughtfully. It doesn't mean we don't have things to learn. It means we are capable of learning more, and that's inspiring! The work gets better when we feel better in the work. A great way to feel happy in the work—and to spread happiness—is to love ourselves through the process of growing and evolving.

Reflection Questions:

- How might you celebrate growth and progress for learners and yourself?
- What is one thought you find yourself coming back to that feels unproductive, and how might you use the cognitive triangle to retrain your brain?

CHAPTER 2

WE ARE NOT PIZZA

*Courage is like a muscle.
We strengthen it by use.*

—RUTH GORDON

When I was six years old, my dad passed away from chronic myeloid leukemia. He was only thirty-three years old when he died. My dad and I had a special bond, and it was difficult to process a loss of that magnitude at such a young age. I can remember keeping shirts with his smell on them in my closet. My mom got me a journal, where I would write about my feelings, and I continued taking dance classes. Dance was a place to forget about loss and fear. It was a place where I could be in the moment. Until it wasn't. As the years went by, I started to become more involved in the dance world. I joined a competitive dance team and would spend six or sometimes seven days a week at the studio, often for three to four hours or more. I lived for the applause of audiences and praise from my instructors. I loved performing in school talent shows and for audiences at malls and senior living communities. I relished winning and collecting trophies at dance competitions. And all of that is fun and can be healthy. I learned a good amount from my time in the dance world. I learned how to be disciplined. I learned how to work well on a team. I learned the importance of hard work and attention to detail. I became a more confident person.

But somewhere along the way, dance became the place where I found value as a human being. When I won competitions, it made me feel like a special person—which means that when I lost competitions, I felt less special. When I received praise from dance instructors, I felt loved and important. When I received criticism, I felt less so. I lived for those gold stars.

The same was true in school. Since I'd learned at an early age that there is a lot about the world that is scary and that we can't control, I became very focused on what I could control. My grades, my behavior, the kinds of comments that would show up on report cards. By the time I reached high school, I was involved in just about every club I could find. I took pride in being involved in school. But it went beyond pride. It made me feel valuable.

This is where the tender distinction lies. That fine line between being proud of yourself and what you accomplish and tying your value as a human being to your performance.

In high school, I had high hopes of becoming a professional dancer. My mom, a hardworking single parent, wanted to support my dream but wanted to ensure that I had a solid backup plan. She told me that I could always move to New York and audition for shows after I earned my college degree. Like many young adults, I struggled with what I would study in college. I ended up pursuing teaching because I'd always enjoyed school and figured maybe I would become a teacher. Though it grew into one, my teaching career did not begin as a pursuit of passion.

Despite my lack of enthusiasm, my early teaching was still fueled by my desire for external validation. And it was exhausting. Kids are honest, and I've grown to love that about them, but when you are a student teacher in a sophomore English class, there is rarely applause or a standing ovation like you see in the movies. I graduated from college and taught high school English language arts for four years. I'm not proud of this, but I chose high school because I thought being a high school teacher would be impressive. I thought it might make other people think I was smart. While that wasn't a great reason, I'm glad I started my teaching career in high school because I learned how to be OK when people didn't applaud me. I learned how to be OK when students didn't enjoy my lesson or complained about my class. I learned that other people are smarter than me—and many times those people are my students.

It took me four years of teaching in a high school classroom to honestly ask myself whether I was enjoying it.

I wasn't.

So, I ventured into the world of middle school, where I was equally humbled but for different reasons. Many of my classes were filled with students who were in a variety of places developmentally. Some students seemed more like elementary kids. Others seemed more like high schoolers, and many fell in the middle. My students showed up with many different needs and expectations, and I fumbled my way through my first year with them.

But middle school saved my teaching career, and it grew me. Middle school is where I learned how to be a better teacher. For lack of better words, middle school kids can be a bit of a lovable mess, hormones all over the place, trying to figure out who they are and want to be. But somewhere in the mess that is middle school, I learned to stop focusing on myself and my performance and to instead focus on truly being present with my students. Suddenly, little moments such as a disciplinary issue or a lesson flop weren't personal and about me. Instead, these moments were rich with possibility for students. There is power in interrupting our thinking to see where our emotions are coming from. I learned that my emotions were coming from a place of viewing student behavior as a personal attack instead of a form of communication. I couldn't help but become deeply curious about students.

I got hooked on studying my students and then trying something new with them to see if it would lead to higher student engagement and performance. Curiosity can be just as valuable as intelligence. Perhaps more valuable because it can lead to deeper levels of learning. Middle school kids made me smarter and more empathetic. It is amazing what happens when we let go of the fear of not being perfect or fear of what others think of us and instead allow ourselves to be fed by learning and growing.

But shortly after my first year as a seventh-grade ELA teacher, perfectionism started creeping in. My students were in the red for their growth on the state test. I cried privately about being a bad teacher and thought about quitting. Luckily, I had a strong teaching partner, Courtney Ward, and together we tried some new approaches with our students. Mainly, I spent time 1:1 conferring with students in my class. We would engage in reading and writing conferences and individual student goal setting, among other strategies. I became less focused on the red and more focused on what I could do in the present. And that next school year, my students were in the yellow for their growth on the state assessment. More importantly, class felt more engaging, and I believe students felt more seen.

The following year, I started incorporating more choices in my class. Students read books they'd selected, and I began using formative instructional practices to inform small-group instruction. That year, my student growth was in the green and my students passed the state test. One of those students hadn't received a proficient score in years. It was very motivating. But it's not all about test scores. What I learned from all this was that I didn't need to be perfect to make a difference. I didn't need accolades from others to be valuable. What mattered more was that I was trying—and when something didn't work, that was an opportunity to get curious and try something else. I was growing professionally and as a human being, which was deeply satisfying. I can attribute a large amount of that growth to a close friend and colleague, Dr. Kim Given, whose classroom was across the hall from mine. Between class periods, we would step into the hallway to greet students and would enjoy meaningful dialogue about what we were trying in our classrooms. It's amazing what three- to four-minute conversations with an educator you trust and deeply admire can do for your professional practice. I still say that those conversations were some of the best professional development I've ever received.

My value of progress over perfection felt more motivating and humanizing. But here is where things get a little tricky. Placing too much of our value on progress isn't healthy either. Needing to feel like we are getting better all the time is a form of perfectionism, especially when we believe we need to get stronger in everything all at once. Perfectionism fosters unrealistic expectations for what we can achieve and feelings of shame when we don't achieve those unrealistic expectations. To this day, this is the type of perfectionism I continue to fight, because when I can't find progress, nothing feels good enough. And when nothing feels good enough, I don't feel good enough.

After four years of teaching middle school and eight total years of teaching, I became an assistant principal. Later, I became an assessment and accountability coordinator—which is a fancy way of saying that it was really hard to make new friends in the schools. The words *assessment* and *accountability* don't tend to be crowd pleasers. During that time, Ohio was rolling out new state tests and testing requirements and making big changes to the teacher evaluation system. We also had new district initiatives and vendor assessments to contend with. This made my job a big one. With nine school buildings and over seven thousand students, I was in charge of supporting major changes. All of this was new to me, and I had no idea what I was doing.

Because so much was new to me, I craved success outside of work. I needed to see progress and to feel in some kind of control. So, I started eating better and exercising. I took pride in my discipline, and I started to see results. After a while, my progress would plateau, and

I would tweak my plan to see more results. But before long, my commitment became an obsession with results. I was no longer concerned with my energy levels, whether my muscles were getting stronger, or whether I was pleased with how I felt in my clothes. I merely wanted to see if I could make the number on the scale go down a little more. I look back at pictures from that time in my life and feel a little sad. I look like someone who wanted to take up as little space as possible. Much of that time in my life is a blur. I was more focused on progress than I was on living a healthy life. That's a level of perfectionism that can be unhealthy.

I share these moments because I'm worried about educators. Some of us want the highest scores. Others want to show that we're getting better in many areas all at once. Some put unhealthy energy into activities outside of school because we feel so overwhelmed inside of it. I've seen veteran teachers filled with crippling fear over an upcoming observation because they don't think they can show their evaluator everything they can do in thirty minutes. They are right. We can't show all that we can do in thirty minutes nor should we have to do this. Administrators need to spend time in classrooms every week so observations are not an event. Teachers and students need to be seen for what they can do beyond a thirty-minute snapshot. Yes to all of that. But we have also got to find a way to care a little less about this kind of stuff. I don't mean care less about our instruction or our students' learning—I mean worry less about what people are thinking about us, less about whether we are going to receive an accomplished rating on our evaluation. It's not worth it. We are more than a rating and our students are more than a number. We are more than one observation. We are more than our accomplishments and our progress or lack thereof. We are people. Human beings with real feelings and complex lives and different lived experiences. There is a big, beautiful world out there that my dad, Greg Lawson, would have loved to experience. I think he would be devastated if I spent most of my life stressed about calories and working late nights to perfect presentations.

Perfectionism steals moments from us. As human beings, we are wired for moments. Moments of connection. Moments of joy. Moments of learning and reflection. Perfectionism keeps us from trying new things and achieving big things because perfectionism tells us that it's not good enough, so we might as well stop trying. I can't be the only person who has fixated on details of presentations, agendas, or things I did or didn't say in meetings. That last one might be my biggest area of struggle. I can spend hours focused on a conversation that I wanted to go differently. It's easy to become so focused on some of these details and the unrealistic standards we have set for ourselves that we shut down and stop moving or taking action. We're our own worst and most damaging critics. In his book *Finish*, Jon Acuff writes, "The problem is that perfectionism magnifies your mistakes and minimizes your progress. It does not believe in incremental success. Perfectionism portrays your goal as a house of cards. If one thing doesn't go perfectly, the whole thing falls apart. The smallest misstep means the entire goal is ruined."[1]

Let's not make sweeping judgments about ourselves or our capabilities. Let's commit to trying. And trying again. If we do this, I think we'll change for the better. I think we'll become more grounded. We'll grow and be happier. I think we will achieve more. Schools will change and, since schools are the epicenter of our community culture, the world will change. No one is ever going to look back at us and our impact and say, "Wow, that educator changed my life because they were perfect." In fact, I once hired a job coach who said something I will never forget. She said, "Meghan, people don't like perfect people." Think about that. First, there are no perfect people. Second, when we work hard at being perfect, we make our work about us and beyond others. We make it seem superhuman. When we don't share our struggles, our learning, our mistakes with other people, we make leading classrooms, schools, and districts something that is beyond other people. We make it something that only perfect people do.

The world doesn't need more perfect people or more people who are focused on winning the approval of others. The world needs rolled-up sleeves and whole hearts. In the book *Innovate inside the Box* by George Couros and Katie Novak, a quote of mine appears: "We don't have to be perfect to make a difference. We need to care deeply about our impact on kids, care deeply about our words, and we need to embrace our humanness."[2]

Being human means understanding that sometimes our brains misfire. As I've previously mentioned, our brains are wired to look for threats. Think about the number of times your heart has raced when there has been no actual threat. Perhaps it's an ambiguous "call me" text from a boss. Perhaps you receive an unexpected visit from an administrator who doesn't come into your room very often. Does anyone else get a little panicky when their phone rings and it's a number they don't know? Whatever it may be, it's amazing how quickly our reptilian brain takes over. And not only do we get startled, but we come up with stories about what's really going on. The text from our boss must mean we did or said the wrong thing, and she's going to tell us. That classroom visit from an administrator is surely happening because they think we're doing a bad job and they need to check up on us.

It's exhausting. I'm tired of it. Aren't you tired of it? Living with the reptilian brain is overwhelming. It certainly has its place—we must learn how to stay safe. But when you get no breaks from looking for the lions in the village, it's too much. Not to mention that an escalated adult cannot deescalate a child. It's quite difficult to lead healthy classrooms and school communities when we are at our wits' end.

The Story I'm Telling Myself

Let me offer you a case in point. During my time as an associate director of curriculum and instruction, I led principals and assistant principals through various aspects of our work. One of those areas included district-approved vendor assessments and state tests. One year, there was a new assistant principal at one of our high schools, and testing was one of her management areas. It was the start of the year, and she was new, and I was newish to my role, and she had many thoughts and questions about spring testing. I remember thinking, "What's with this person? She keeps bringing up assessments that won't happen until six months from now. Is she trying to make me feel behind? Is she trying to make me look bad in front of the team?" I continued to feel agitated and a bit annoyed by all of it. One day I messaged her the following (this is how we often communicated—I realize now that a phone call or in-person conversation would have been more appropriate for this): "The story I'm telling myself is that you think I'm behind in my work on testing." She quickly replied, "The story I'm telling myself is that I need to prove to you how on top of this work I am since I am new to the team and to administration."

Ah. OK, we were getting somewhere. First of all, this was during my deep dive into every Brené Brown book ever written—so I was feeling pretty proud of that "story I'm telling myself" language. To this day, I think it's a great way to be honest about what we are thinking and feeling without making the other person feel attacked. It also invites the other person into a conversation. They can validate whether they see it that way and/or share the story they are telling themselves. We can teach our students to use this type of language with us and with each other. In this case, we had two female administrators feeling like they weren't good enough and like they had to prove to others that they were capable. We were able to speak clearly and directly with each other about how we were feeling and, more importantly, how we were impacting each other. This made the work a lot easier because we could spend less time in the worry zone. I'm glad I reached out, and I'm glad we were clear with each other about our feelings and intentions. Higher levels of trust and communication improved the quality of our work together moving forward.

Feedforward

In that same role, in the previous school year, I was leading a team of mostly male principals and assistant principals. At that time, I had never been a principal, and I was younger than most of the men on the team. I spent that first school year in the role mostly listening and writing thoughts and ideas down in a spiral notebook. I wanted to get this right, and I wanted them to see that I respected their experiences and leadership. We gathered monthly for what we called CIA meetings: curriculum, instruction, and assessment. We were in the CIA! I really should have gotten us some sunglasses—it sounded so cool. The story I told myself about these meetings was that I wasn't qualified to do much beyond listening, writing down what they said, and reflecting those thoughts back to them. That type of negative self-talk did not serve me or the team well. At our final meeting in June, I asked for feedback on how these meetings could better address their needs the following school year. I will never forget what one of the principals (who I consider a friend to this day) said clearly and kindly: "You know, it feels like we do a lot of talking in these meetings, but we don't make any decisions. If we are going to spend this time away from our buildings, it will be important that we make decisions and get to the action."

As a self-proclaimed doer, that was hard to hear. It confirmed my worst fear about being underqualified. It confirmed thoughts I was having about being ineffective and wasting their time. I had a choice. I could question myself for the rest of that summer and curl up in a ball, or I could use that growth-evoking feedback to make changes. So, I read books about how to lead meetings that get things done. I read books about creating meaningful learning experiences too. I reminded myself that it was not too late to become really good at this part of my job. And for the next two years, we did some of the best work of my career. Together. And much of that work was decided on and accomplished in those meetings. We changed the way we weighted grades and moved to research-aligned start times in our middle and high schools. We developed new schedules that gave high school teachers collaboration time during their workday. We moved away from valedictorian and salutatorian in favor of a Latin honors system that recognized the achievements of more students. We removed class rank from transcripts. We did work that centered the humanity of children. We did work that we believed would support an environment where students could enjoy the learning process, take more classes that interested them, and focus less on how they were performing in comparison to their peers. We simply listened to the voices of students, staff, and community members and took action.

We did good, imperfect work. And it didn't matter that it wasn't perfect because it was good work done for the right reasons with learners at the center.

And I can't help but wonder if we could have done it without that June CIA meeting. I chose to internalize that important, difficult-to-hear feedback in a feedforward way. In her blog post "Moving from Feedback to Feedforward," Jennifer Gonzalez explains, "When we give feedforward, instead of rating and judging a person's performance in the past, we focus on their development in the future." We, as educators, are constantly receiving feedback, much of it unsolicited. There are many people who believe they know how to do our jobs well because they themselves were students once. We work with students who do not have fully developed frontal lobes and sometimes struggle to share what they think about us in ways that feel constructive. We work with administrators who may or may not be in our classrooms much and who evaluate us according to rubrics that may or may not adequately represent what we feel is important in our profession.

The key is knowing the difference between critical feedback and mere criticism or negativity. Critical feedforward is given by people who are invested in our growth and/or the greater good of our schools and organizations. Criticism and negativity are more about tearing down than building up. When we understand the difference, we can discern what we will allow to inform our next moves.

And when we ourselves are giving feedforward, we can consider how to do so in a way that focuses on building up and on the future rather than the past. Here's an example: An administrator or instructional coach is working with a teacher who feels like peer-to-peer dialogue is getting stale. Upon spending time in the classroom and observing the dialogue, this administrator or coach might say, "The next time students do a turn and talk, I wonder what would happen if they got out of their seats, stayed standing, and talked to someone they don't normally sit next to in class?" (Only ask an "I wonder" question if you genuinely wonder—otherwise, it can come off as condescending.) The administrator or coach could also simply ask the teacher what they might try next time to increase student engagement during class dialogue. The last approach might be a great place to start. We don't want to steal reflection and learning moments away from educators.

The same feedforward framing goes for students as well. We need to offer feedforward *during* the learning process instead of feedback only at the end of an assessment, unit, or quarter. Students need hope-giving information on their performance. They need to receive those insights when they still have time to do something with that information. Otherwise, all they get is the finality of a grade. Here's an example: When conferring with a student who relies on simple sentence structure, a teacher might say, "I wonder if the writing would sound different if you combined some of your sentences with a comma and conjunction. It would be fun to read the sentences out loud both ways and hear how the writing changes—let's play around with it!"

Opening the Lines of Communication

The more time I spend in schools, the more I realize how critical it is to invite and listen to the voices of our students and to truly honor the feedback and feedforward they give us. If you truly want to know how things are working for students, ask them. Student voice is one of the most underutilized resources in our schools. Ask, and when psychological safety is in place, they will tell you. And when they tell you, listen. I find that students have such smart, practical insights and ideas, and they are invested in making school better because they're the ones who have to live the experiences we create every day.

When you frame student feedback that way, it may still be difficult to hear, but it doesn't feel critical or negative. It feels incredibly productive and inspiring. And the more we ask students, the more normal it feels. One day when I was teaching middle school English, I noticed a student was keeping a tally on a sheet of paper during my mini-lesson. I moved closer and discovered that he was keeping a tally of the number of "likes" and "ums" that I used while speaking. My initial reaction internally was to take this feedback personally. Especially since, as you might imagine, he was laughing to himself. When I asked him to give me the paper, his laughter turned to terror. I wondered how I should handle this. I wanted to open our lines of communication and keep our relationship intact while also being clear about the ways I prefer to receive feedback. When class ended, I connected with him individually. I explained that this was very important feedback for me. It truly was, and quite honestly, it has made me much more aware even to this day of pausing when I speak versus using filler words. I also explained that it is important for me to know when something I am doing as a teacher is distracting from his learning. I told him that in the future,

I would appreciate it if he would share the feedback with me directly. Finally, to try to lighten the mood since he appeared embarrassed, I smiled, chuckled, and explained, "I didn't realize that perfection was the standard we were setting in this course. I will remember that the next time I grade one of your papers." While I was kidding with him, I think I would have avoided that last part if I could go back and redo that conversation. Too often our students don't share their feedback for that very reason: fear of retaliation. Kidding or not, it's important that our students are clear about how much we value and appreciate their perspective.

In fact, in general, the more time we spend asking people for feedback, the less scary feedback becomes. It's merely a conversation between people who care about each other and the mission. When we consistently celebrate the good together, too, we can sense that it's not all bad. We must train our minds to see the good that's all around and the good that's within us too. And when you see the good, speak it. Write a handwritten note. Send a text. Make the call. Anything that shows people you see them and that there is so much good there. That way, when they hear something that feels a little hard, they'll be less likely to build entire narratives or identities around the heavy stuff.

As human beings, we have limits. We can't work on making everything better at one time. We must remember that about ourselves, our students, and our staff. We are human beings, not human *doings*. We cannot do it all or do it all well. So, we must know ourselves and what matters most to us. Let's make what matters most as good as we can. Change what we can. We will figure out the rest later.

Leading Change Scared

Our world continues to change at an increasingly rapid pace. Therefore, we must continue to change and try new things. As George Couros says, "Change is the opportunity to do something amazing." He doesn't say that change is an opportunity to do something perfectly or that change is easy. It's an opportunity. And when we take that opportunity to make a change, whether it's a change to an instructional practice or a change to our school system, there is risk involved. We will fail at some part of it, and we will learn from those mistakes. There will be people who don't like what we are doing too. I've seen a quote that's usually attributed to Steve Jobs: "If you want to make everyone happy, don't be a leader. Sell ice cream." I've also seen that meme that says, "You can't make everyone happy. You are not pizza." Whatever the saying or meme may be, efforts to make everyone happy are a fool's errand. Not only is it impossible, but it's also dissatisfying. I'm learning not to hustle after my own worth. Instead, I decide what I believe is right. I'm hustling after the things that feel really, really good for learners.

I'm also learning that while we cannot make everyone happy, we can ensure people feel seen and heard. Which goes a long way. So often, we stress over how people will feel about a change we present to them. In reality, we should focus on whether they've been part of the change process. If they're part of the process, they can feel invested or at least have the opportunity to dissent before the change is made official. It's human nature to reject new plans and ideas that we didn't know were coming or that we had no part in developing. We often expect people to accept changes and be as excited about them as we are, but we've had much more time to consider or influence the change ourselves. We must learn to socialize ideas and to share those ideas before they're carried out. We must get more comfortable talking through what I call the sacrificial draft—work that's not done, not pretty, or not perfect. There is power in people seeing something unfinished. It makes them more likely to offer their honest feedback. If they only see the work at the end, they may think we're simply "checking the box" by showing it to them. We must be better about talking through ideas and drafts with staff members, students, parents, and community members, in small groups, in big groups, and in 1:1 chats in the hallway. We must get more comfortable with having visitors in our classrooms when we are trying new things. Being a learner in front of others, including students, is important in helping others understand the value of learning and learning from mistakes.

We must learn to do it scared. Because it's scary to put something in front of people when you think they may have a strong reaction to it. But it's a lot easier to push through the fear when you believe with your whole heart that you are doing the right thing for the right reason, which is to support the growth and development of children and educators. If we don't stand for anything, we stand for nothing. It's scary to let other people see our teaching when we haven't perfected the lesson or tried a particular thing with students before. We must find ways to push through the fear. It's the only way to deepen our collective sense of humanity and make our schools better places to learn and work.

In my school district, when we were changing our approach to weighted grades, class rank, and start times, it was scary. And I mean really scary. The work started on committees. We socialized in many, many different settings with various groups of people. We surveyed people. We spoke at board meetings. We talked about it—a lot. And even then, the night before the proposed changes were up for board approval, I started to panic. I started to feel like I couldn't breathe. I was stuck in my chair, frozen in fear. So, I called my job coach. This coach was someone I had hired to help me figure out what I wanted to do with my life—which didn't quite work out. Instead, she helped me get really good at what I was doing in the now: change work. She said to me, "What is the worst thing that could happen?" I said, "Parents will come to this meeting with pitchforks and demand that I get fired." She replied, "OK, and then what?" I thought for a second and said, "And then the local media will show up, and people all over the city will have an opportunity to think bad things about me and my work." Almost without missing a beat, she stated, "Great, so then what happens? What's the worst thing that could happen after that?" I wondered for a second and then found my worst fear. I said, "And then I will be fired."

I will never forget what she said to me at that moment. "Do you believe what you are doing is in the best interest of students?" Without a moment's pause, I said confidently, "Yes." She explained, "So, what if you get fired? You believe in what you are doing. If you lose your job, you will find another one."

It may sound odd, but I needed to hear that. I needed to hear that no matter what, I was going to be OK. If I did work I believed the world needed, I was going to be OK. Things were going to work out. Learning to be our own champion in this work is important.

Doing hard things doesn't mean that we don't do them scared. It means that we feel the fear, identify where it is coming from, and proceed from there. We must pay attention to our thoughts. Too often, the people who know the right thing to do and have the skills to do it, don't. And too often, it's because we are afraid, we feel small, or we don't trust our instincts.

If we aren't a bit uncomfortable—and if people in our organizations aren't questioning our work and feeling a bit uncomfortable, too—are we working on anything that really matters? And isn't that what we all went into education to do? Work that really matters? I'm not saying that we shouldn't be mindful of our community's readiness level for various changes. What I am saying is that if nothing changes, nothing changes.

We cannot perform ourselves into higher self-worth. We do not become more valuable by getting everything checked off our to-do lists or by getting approval and credit from others. We are deeply feeling humans having a deeply human experience. So, let's allow ourselves to do the best we can and quiet some of the unhelpful noise.

The Damage of Doing It All

I spent my first year in a central office role serving others as best I could. Having just left a role as an assistant principal, I could appreciate the rapid pace of a school environment and the grind of a school day. It's challenging. As an assessment and accountability coordinator, I tried to do everything I could to make testing and data more manageable for principals. I wanted them to see that I could add value, especially since I was in a central office position that appeared to be "an add." You know exactly what I'm talking about. We've all been there, raising eyebrows at positions that seem further and further from the classroom. I wanted to prove that I was capable and reliable and helpful and needed. I did everything I could to ensure that principals and staff didn't have to worry about anything related to testing and data. I went into my evaluation at the end of that school year exhausted from proving myself, and my supervisor gave me some important feedback that changed me forever as a leader. She said, "You've learned and achieved so much this year, but what have you taught people to do for themselves?" The truth was—not much. I had not shown them how I had done any of it, and I hadn't grown their ability to do the work themselves. If something had happened to me that day, they would have been no better off than they were before I arrived. I spent so much of my time doing for other people that I had forgotten leadership is not only about removing barriers. It is also about developing people so they can do for themselves.

This happens in our classrooms too. It comes from a good place, but it's often not a great practice. If we make all the decisions and do all the things for learners, then we have put leadership out of reach. Learners don't get to see what they can accomplish themselves. If we protect learners from making decisions and trying new things, we take learning away from them. When we take learning away from students and staff, we take growth away from them, and we take away the happiness that comes from internalizing that growth. And I know that none of us went into education to take happiness away. In the foreword of the book *Empower: What Happens When Students Own Their Learning* by John Spencer and A. J. Juliani, George Couros perfectly states as much: "Your legacy as an educator is always determined by what your students do. You change the world by empowering your students to do the same."[3] We are here to make other people feel like they can expand themselves and accomplish things they never thought possible.

There is magic inside every imperfect human being. Our greatest job as educators is to unearth that magic, celebrate it, and leverage it for the greater good of our classrooms, schools, and communities.

As George Couros said, "We must make the positives so loud that the negatives are almost impossible to hear." He didn't say we wouldn't hear the negatives at all. What he said is that we need to flip the script because right now, it feels like we have to work really hard to hear the positives. What would happen if, instead, we had to work really hard to hear the unconstructive negatives because those positives were just so energizing and motivating? Perfectionism and the obsession with results steals our creativity, our playfulness, and our ability to enjoy our work. Focusing on what is going well makes us feel capable, energized, and hopeful that we can make tomorrow better than today. Yes, we must hear constructive, difficult truths. This is where change often starts. However, it's easier to hear those difficult truths when we are also affirmed by what is going well.

Reflection Questions:

- What is one area where you find yourself overly concerned with perfection or progress? Where might those feelings be coming from?
- What would you do in your classroom or school if you knew you could not fail? Is that something really good for learners? If so, can you find a way to do it?

- How might you replace perfection with connection in your classroom or school? Instead of worrying about how things look to others, what might it look like to be fully present in the moment with learners?

- What matters most to you? How might you remind yourself of your mission and priorities when the work and expectations of others feel overwhelming?

- The people who need love the most often ask for it in the most unloving ways. How might you celebrate the good of those around you in a way that feels caring and authentic to you?

- What is something you've been busy doing for learners that they could do for themselves?

CHAPTER 3

RIDICULOUSLY IN CHARGE

*The best way to change someone else's behavior
is to change our own behavior first.*

—LAINIE ROWELL

In the previous chapter, I discussed the need to push past fear, criticism, and self-defeating thoughts—not as a way to avoid doing difficult tasks, but to create space to pursue the things that really matter to us. To truly be our own champions, we must set boundaries and be honest with ourselves and others about what we are willing or not willing to take on at any given time. We need to recognize that when we say we don't have time for things, often what we really mean is that some things just aren't a priority for us right now.

And that's OK.

Many of us don't like to word it that way because being honest about our priorities requires vulnerability. Being honest about what is or isn't a priority puts difficult truths into perspective. Sometimes, it just sounds bad that something isn't a priority, especially if that something is family or taking care of ourselves. But hearing ourselves say that is the first step in recognizing that perhaps some of our priorities need to be adjusted. Other times, hearing ourselves say that something isn't a priority is validating. It confirms for us that taking on that additional workload or joining that book club truly isn't a priority right now. Being clear about that boundary can be an important way to honor our time and energy.

It is humanly impossible to give maximum effort in all that we do.

And yet, this may be one of the most destructive "virtues" that we learned as a child and that we are passing along to children in our schools. There is simply no way to give 100 percent in every moment of the day and in every area of our life. But many of us try to live up to those expectations. Those unrealistic expectations we have for ourselves. And children sit in classrooms trying to live up to those expectations and failing at it every day because it is not humanly possible. Not everything is worth our highest level of effort.

Unfortunately, many of us are quietly going through our day feeling ashamed. We feel ashamed that we didn't give maximum effort in all areas of our work or home life. And you know what shame does? It makes us tired and quiet and closed off. It can actually make us feel so unworthy that the areas that are worth maximum effort cannot be attended to because we are exhausted and defeated. Many of us have become so enthralled by notions of full-time maximum effort that we've forgotten to ask ourselves whether maximum effort is the appropriate amount of effort. I love what Liz Forkin Bohannon has to say about this in her book, *Beginner's Pluck*: "What is the least amount of time/energy/resources I can put into this concept/idea/dream before I can put it out into the universe and actually start getting real-life feedback that will enable me to make it even better?"[1] When appropriate, the sooner we can put that unfinished sacrificial draft in front of others, the sooner we will receive insights that will improve the quality of the work. Less agonizing over getting it right the first time and more curiosity about what we can learn from others along the way.

Work Hours

A number of my friends who are educators pride themselves on their late hours. They pride themselves on attending all of their students' after-school events. They wear the amount of hours they spend catching up on grading as a badge of honor. They stand tall when they tell you that they came into school on Sunday to catch up on things and do some lesson planning.

I'm not here to make them feel ashamed. Only they know what is right for them and where they want to spend their maximum effort. But what I will say is that if you are working long hours because you think those are the actions required of a good teacher, a legacy educator . . . If you are doing those things simply because you want other people to think you are a hard worker and one of the best, I encourage you to take a step back and question where you find your worth as a human being.

I do not think twice when I see a staff member leaving at their contracted time. This is not because I don't have high standards and expectations for learning. It's because I have learned that my worth as a human being and professional do not come from what other people think of me. So I, too, leave at my contracted time when I can. I have a 4:30 p.m. appointment with my personal trainer daily. So, I have to leave by 4:00 p.m. in order to make that appointment. It is a priority for me. My health and well-being are a priority for me. I have said no to after-school happy hours. I have said no to some meetings. I have missed phone calls and asked if I can call back later.

I say no so I can say yes to myself and my well-being. What's amazing is that after that hour of working out, I am energized. I often go home and actually want to do more work. I typically spend another hour or so working when I get home from that workout. Not because I have to. Because I want to. And some days, I don't. Some days I'm tired, and whatever work I have left to do, if it's important, will be waiting for me tomorrow.

Email. Sigh.

Which brings me to email. Too many years of my career were spent worrying about email and being of service to my email. I would check my email all day long. And because I was checking it so often, I missed some moments with my students. They were talking to me, but I wasn't fully listening to them because I was thinking about a stressful email that was sitting in my inbox. I can remember sitting at a major league baseball play-off game, worrying about an email from an angry parent, working on that perfect reply on my phone. I don't remember much if any of that game, and I haven't had the opportunity to attend a baseball play-off game since.

I've learned that email pulls me out of the present moment and into someone else's moment. Once I realized the effect email had on me, I changed my habits. Now I check my email in the morning, in the middle of my day (sometimes), and always at the end of my day. Otherwise, I figure if something is urgent, it will find me outside of my email. I'm not saying that this is a best practice or an effective practice. It's simply what I need. Email is not a high priority for me. Being fully in the present moment with staff and students is my highest priority during the workday. Now, checking email every day does matter to me. Because responding to people within twenty-four hours matters to me, delivering high levels of customer service matters to me. But responding instantaneously is not my priority. Not to mention it sort of sends the message that we're just waiting around for someone who needs a response. And that's not reality for most of us.

Our students don't need teachers who do everything perfectly and instantaneously at a high level. Our students need teachers who are deeply interested in them. Our school staff need administrators who are so interested in them and who care so deeply about them as human beings, professionals, and learners that they don't want to spend their days in their office at their computer. They need administrators who want to be in classrooms, in hallways, at lunch, and at recess celebrating good work and being a part of solutions. Our students need teachers who are so interested in what they have to say and how they're doing that they want to spend time with them.

At least, that's how I see it. Those are some of my priorities. If I had to choose between an administrator or teacher who exuded joy and presence with learners and one who responded immediately to emails and phone calls, I would choose the person who prioritized time with people. So many issues that arise during the day are resolved when we work on them in person, together.

I've learned that not all people see it that way. Some people send emails when they are upset or want to resolve a matter. But usually this is not how I work. I prefer phone calls and in-person meetings so we can hear each other's tone of voice and read body language. It's not that I say no when someone wishes to engage. That would be rude and uncalled for, and often those emails raise valid concerns. Instead, I say no to the idea that I have to respond in that same format. I often reply with something along the lines of:

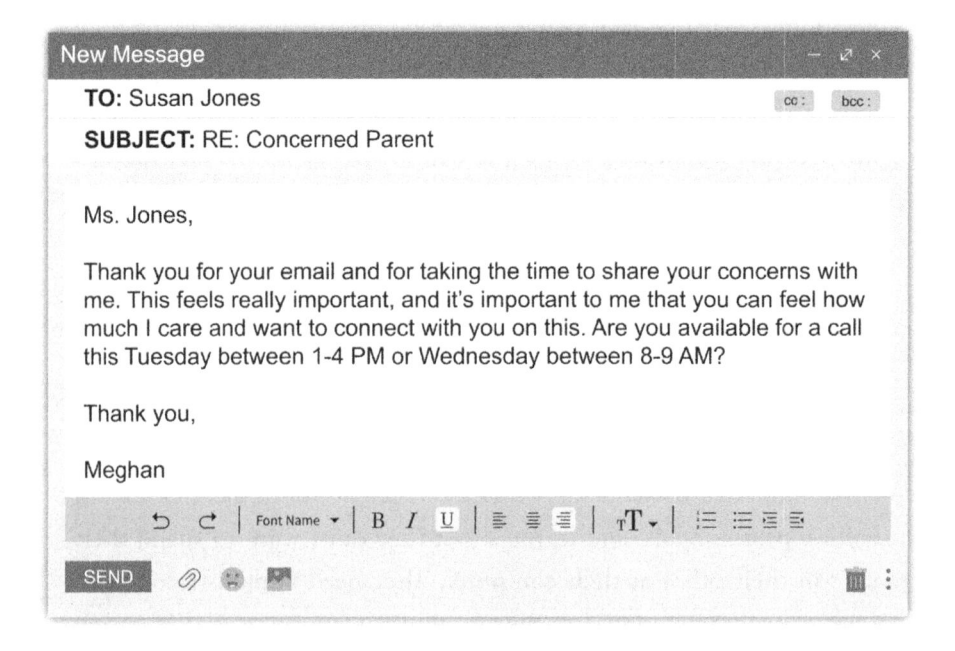

New Message

TO: Susan Jones

SUBJECT: RE: Concerned Parent

Ms. Jones,

Thank you for your email and for taking the time to share your concerns with me. This feels really important, and it's important to me that you can feel how much I care and want to connect with you on this. Are you available for a call this Tuesday between 1-4 PM or Wednesday between 8-9 AM?

Thank you,

Meghan

Sometimes, we will work on something together on that call that requires a follow-up email to summarize the plan moving forward. But rarely has anyone complained about the fact that I want to connect via phone or in person. I get a lot of time back when I work this way, and I feel better about the way I show up for people. It takes a serious amount of time to respond in writing to someone experiencing escalated emotions because we must be careful with every word, our formatting, and our punctuation to ensure that our tone is not misinterpreted and that we do not upset the individual further. Often what we type in those emails can still be triggering despite our best efforts.

So, I say no to that. And I say yes to doing it in a way that feels right to me.

Too Many Standards

Healthy email habits are one small example to illustrate the power of saying no. I wonder what would happen if we were to apply this thinking to our instructional practices and the way we lead our classrooms.

There was a time when I tried to consume as many education-related books as possible. I thought that the best way to become a good teacher and a good leader would be to read any book I could get my hands on. I enjoyed many of those books. But I was consuming books at such a high volume and taking in ideas at such a rapid rate that I constantly felt like I needed to change many of my instructional or leadership practices—at once. I wasn't able to reflect deeply because I was rushing from book to book with all that content floating around in my mind at a superficial level. (My blood pressure is going up as I write that!) But I've learned that just because someone wrote something in a book—this book included—does not mean it's what's best for you or that you need to make a bunch of changes right now.

Too often, teachers feel like they should change their instruction in big ways and all at once. As Patrick Lencioni said, "When everything is important, then nothing is."[2] It's not humanly possible to change everything at the same time and do it all with maximum effort. Unfortunately, we often unintentionally send these messages to teachers in our meetings and communications. Understandably, some veteran teachers see this as "flavor of the month" leadership and adopt a "this too shall pass" mindset because it's overwhelming and exhausting.

Rather than rush recklessly to new methods, we must be honest with ourselves about how the students in our classrooms are doing and what methods will best meet their needs. We also must stop villainizing practices simply because they've been around for a long time. In some instances, and in moderation, those practices may be working for students. It's not all or nothing. For example, there are times when our students need explicit instruction as a class. Other times, they need explicit instruction in small groups. Neither method is the one true way. It's about paying attention to each of our students and how they respond to the learning. What I do know to be true is that doing anything for long periods of time can be difficult—not only for students but also adults. Most of us need our learning experiences to be chunked into segments. However, there are many methods, old and new, that can be effective with students. We can't make smart decisions for the students we serve if we're fixated on whether we used every instructional practice deemed effective in one lesson.

This brings me to state standards. My apologies to those of you who may get itchy when I say this: We must say no to covering every standard with the same level of gusto. We cannot give 100 percent to every learning standard. It cannot be done. Students don't have the capacity for it either. It's too much. I wonder what would happen if we were to cut our curriculum in half—as a team of professionals. I'm sure that statement will elicit some shock and awe. Perhaps I don't mean throwing out certain standards entirely but rather prioritizing standards. What if we got together and asked ourselves, "What is really, really important to the long-term success and well-being of our students?" What would happen if we taught those skills deeply and with great care while honoring the humanity of learners? What would happen if students didn't know every term or didn't spend much time on every standard, but they knew how to think deeply, feel deeply, care deeply? What if we said no to obsessing over state test results and said yes to obsessing over raising competent, deeply thinking, and deeply feeling humans? I'm not saying we stop caring about standards or stop teaching standards entirely. I'm merely wondering what it would look like if we stopped obsessing over *all* standards. State assessments are one metric. I'm not saying that metric doesn't matter. I'm saying that it's simply a metric and often what matters most is more difficult to measure. If we spend more time on the standards that we, as a community of practice, have determined are high priority, we can make space for meaningful learning and experiences. Perhaps then students could focus on asking more thoughtful questions, solving more problems they care about, and interacting in meaningful ways with the world outside of school. We could focus on nurturing students to be curious learners, critical thinkers, and strong readers, writers, collaborators, and communicators. The world might change. Our scores on state assessments might actually improve versus plummet. It's the power of no that gives us the opportunity to say yes.

The pressure of prioritizing standards can be overwhelming in and of itself because the decisions about where we spend more of our time in the classroom are vital for student learning and future success. Additionally, it is mission critical that all students have access to a guaranteed and viable curriculum. This is why it's important that we make these decisions together as a community of practice, whatever that may mean in your content area, course, grade level, and school system. In the book *Energize Your Teams*, the authors share the following example of how this decision-making process might work: "Ted Horrell and his colleagues in Shelby County, Tennessee, translated criteria Ainsworth (2013) developed into an easy to remember acronym. Using the

R.E.A.L. criteria (readiness, endurance, assessed, and leverage), teachers collaborate as to whether they should consider a particular standard a priority."[3]

In short, I've summarized what the R.E.A.L. criteria encompasses:[4]

> **READINESS:** This standard is critical for success in the next grade level or course.
> **ENDURANCE:** The skills from this standard are useful beyond a single unit or assessment.
> **ASSESSED:** We are confident this standard appears in upcoming state or national assessments. (I personally would add "in a significant or meaningful way.")
> **LEVERAGE:** The learning connected to this standard will support student success across content disciplines.

Certainly, aspects of this conversation will be subject to opinion, and we will need to work through disagreements. However, this rich conversation can lead to important decisions. When we thoughtfully sort standards to determine which standards are low, medium, or high priority, we are equipped with the information needed to prioritize our precious instructional time. With this information at hand, we can now spend time as a team building clear learning targets, defining mastery, and making instructional and assessment decisions for priority standards only. This takes time and hard work. There is no reason to make it harder by trying to do this work with standards we believe matter less.

If I'm fortunate enough to have educators read this book, this chapter is asking for it. It's asking for hate and pushback. And that's OK. Because maybe I'm wrong. I'm simply begging us to question the current system of school we have in place. I'm asking us to question all the things we keep saying yes to. I'm asking us to question all the things about school that we permit and therefore promote. Maybe my ideas are bad ideas. But sometimes hearing a bad idea leads us to a better one, and I'm simply trying to start this conversation because it matters. We can't continue adding more and more and more.

Stress & Rest

Let's be brave enough to question our own systems. For those of us who are overwhelmed and overworked, what systems have we put in place personally that we could change? Are we struggling to get caught up on our grading because all students' papers across class periods are due on the same day? I remember talking to a high school senior who was befuddled by this. He said, "We've been waiting for weeks to get our papers back from our teacher. She's always complaining about how much grading she has to do. And I can't help but think, 'Yeah, but aren't you the one who is assigning all of this work?'" Maybe it's not the due dates but the way we are grading. Maybe it's not the grading but the amount of writing we are collecting. Maybe it's something else entirely.

The point is that we often have much more agency in our work and in our schools than we care to admit. It's easy to blame outside forces. Many outside forces certainly don't make it easy. But there is much more that we can influence. We can be "ridiculously in charge," as Dr. Henry Cloud would put it.[5] We can be ridiculously in charge of ourselves. We can be ridiculously in charge of our work and our well-being. We can be ridiculously in charge of the way we make our students feel in school every day. We can be ridiculously in charge of how we make our colleagues feel at work every day.

We can be ridiculously in charge of our time by being ridiculously in charge of our priorities. We say yes or we say no to much that comes our way. To make the kind of impact we hope to make on our schools and therefore our communities and our world, we must be honest with ourselves about what really matters to us as individuals. We can be ridiculously in charge of our impact by being clear about our boundaries.

We can also be ridiculously in charge of our rest. Rest is a critical part of all work. As Brad Stulberg and Steve Magness state in their book *Peak Performance*, "Stress + rest = growth. This equation holds true regardless of what you are trying to grow."[6] It's not that all stress is bad. It's inevitable when we are working on something important to us. It's that we can't grow at optimal levels if we are constantly busy with our stress. We must build in rest for both ourselves and our students. This is no small feat in our hustle culture. When I'm sitting on the couch, I feel like I need to be doing something, but when I'm busy doing things, I really wish I was relaxing on my couch. The struggle is real! Stulberg and Magness go on to say, "In a society that glorifies grinding, short-term gains and pushing to extremes, it takes guts to rest."[7] We all know we need it, and our students need it too. We need to get over the fear of what other people will think when we incorporate a little rest into our schedules. So what if someone sees your high school classroom playing a quick game for a brain break? So what if someone learns that you binge watched a TV show or spent an entire Sunday afternoon reading a novel? How lovely! Rest is not separate from work. It is an essential component.

Reflection Questions:

- How might you say no to something you've been saying yes to so you can prioritize what feels right for you, your work, and your students?

- What tweaks can you make to your work habits to give yourself back some time?

- How might you incorporate more rest into your schedule and student schedules?

- How might your community of practice adjust the curriculum to ensure there is enough space to nurture meaningful learning?

CHAPTER 4

MOSQUITO MOVES

If you think you're too small to make a difference, you haven't spent the night with a mosquito.

—DALAI LAMA

When we set goals as educators, we often set them *big*. I'm not saying that we shouldn't have big goals or big dreams personally and professionally. But what happens to many of us, particularly those with perfectionist tendencies, is that we go really big and push really hard toward those goals until one day we find ourselves unable to keep up with that thing we said we were going to do every day. We get tired or our tendencies get in the way. Since we haven't built a system that honors our tendencies, and since it's just so big and unmanageable, some of us get discouraged and quit trying.

Tendencies isn't meant to sound like a completely fixed construct. It is simply an observation of self. For example, I feel the most awake and mentally alert later in the day, while others feel sharp in the morning. I do not do my workouts in the morning for this reason. Some people have asked me how it is that I go to work out every day after work. It's because this is the time in the day when I have the most energy for physical exercise. We must be honest with ourselves about our tendencies to set ourselves up for success. Even so, there will be times when we fail. There will be times when something comes up, or we don't perform our best. That's part of being human, but what's critical is how we respond when this occurs. Those achieving great things aren't doing them perfectly every day. It's their commitment to continuing, even when it feels a bit monotonous, that often leads to their success.

Jon Acuff talks about this in his book *Finish*. In chapter 1, he refers to "the day after perfect."[1] Basically, the day after perfect is that first day you don't do what you said you were going to do. And since the streak is broken, and you can no longer hang your hat on the ideal of perfection, it's tempting to quit.

Cut Goals in Half

The sooner the day after perfect creeps up on us, the more likely it is that our goal is too big. So, Acuff explains, "Cut your goal in half."[2] If you know you need to drink more water, and the water you're consuming comes from your coffee or tea, it's tempting to jump right into drinking a gallon of water a day. However, drinking thirty-two ounces a day for an entire year will lead to a higher water intake than drinking a gallon for six days and going back to only coffee or tea. At first, even thirty-two ounces of water a day might feel like a leap. But look at your daily schedule: Can you drink water after your morning workout and replace one soda at lunch with water? Suddenly you're on track with a system that supports your lifestyle. As James Clear says in his book, *Atomic Habits*, "You don't rise to the level of your goals, you fall to the level of your systems."[3] Habit formation is systems work. Those habits don't form in a day; they form in a less glamorous way through small daily moves done consistently over time.

When we make those daily moves consistently, we can be proud, and being proud positively shifts how we view ourselves: "I'm the kind of person who keeps promises to myself." This can be a really beautiful thing, as long as we also offer ourselves compassion when circumstances cause us to get off track.

Our goals and systems need to align with who we are as individuals. We are less likely to pursue goals and stick with systems that don't align with what motivates us. I'm less likely to drink water for the sake of organ health if I'm not interested in organ health. Not that we don't all want healthy organs, but wanting something and being motivated by it are two different things. Maybe I'm more likely to drink water because it can boost my energy levels or because it can make me look less tired around my eyes. An honest motive aligned with a system that honors our tendencies is a great way to support small moves over time that can make a big impact.

And when I say small, you might be surprised at just how small yet impactful the moves can be. In the book *A Billion Hours of Good*, Chris Field talks about how fourteen minutes is roughly 1 percent of a day.[4] I bet I spend well over fourteen minutes a day on social media. What would happen if I shifted fourteen minutes a day into something really good for myself? I'm not saying that I'm quitting social media. I'm just saying that I bet if I were to put a little more time somewhere else instead, good things would happen.

The Power of 1 Percent in the Classroom

The same holds true for the classroom. If fourteen minutes is 1 percent of a full day in our life, then 4.5 minutes is 1 percent of a 7.5-hour workday. And if we teach, say, in fifty-minute periods, then thirty seconds is 1 percent of each class period. How might we take thirty seconds of each class period to improve the experience and educational outcomes of our students?

Think thirty seconds isn't long enough to make a difference? Think again. Think about any little video you've found on the internet. Those can make a big difference in the moment. If I see a funny animal video, my day is instantly brighter! Often those little clips are no longer than thirty seconds. Still think thirty seconds is short? Try holding a plank or doing burpees for thirty seconds. Thirty-second decisions can be very meaningful. In fact, in certain situations, thirty seconds can be the difference between life and death.

Maybe you're a classroom teacher and you're wondering how you might spend thirty seconds of each class period differently. Maybe you're wondering how you might spend 4.5 minutes of your workday differently. Celebrating the good is a great place to start. Imagine looking at your roster of students and choosing one student each day to focus on and offer thirty-second feedback to (mentioned in chapter 1). If you're an instructional coach or principal, imagine keeping a roster with staff names and offering one person a day thirty-second feedback. Once you're through your list, do it again and again and again.

In doing so, you're not just amplifying the good for students and staff, though that's wonderful. You are not just reinforcing the behaviors and mindsets you wish for all learners—which, again, is wonderful. What you're also doing is training your brain. You are training your brain to see the good. You are forming new habits one small move at a time, and before you know it, celebrating the good with genuine spirit and specificity will become a habit that doesn't require much energy. As I mentioned in chapter 1, when we train our brain to see the good, when we make small moves to be more positive, we become more productive. The same is true for those we serve. Receiving positive thirty-second feedback helps others access their greatest potential as well.

This means that perhaps the world isn't changed through grand gestures. As my friend, educational leader and author Lauren Kaufman, once told me, "There will be small moments, small wins, and small obstacles on the path that can seem like they are not enough to bring a vision to fruition. But they add up to the big things that we truly need to accomplish." Maybe the world is changed by groups of people who say they are willing to get 1 percent better each day. Imagine if we all made that kind of a commitment. Our schools would change. Our communities would change. The world would change, and it would be change that is sustainable over time because we all committed a very manageable 1 percent of a day or workday or class period.

We don't need ideal conditions to pursue the 1 percent. When schools were shut down in March of 2020, I was an elementary principal. I loved to greet students at the door in the morning, talk with kids at lunch, and play with kids at recess. Like all of you, I had to change the way that I used my time and the ways that I connected with kids. I would call home on birthdays and sing "Happy Birthday" to students—many times I could hear their parents giggling in the background because, well, I'm not a singer. But what I lack in talent, I make up for with showmanship. I would schedule virtual meetings with a student who had been going through some hard times with her family. I learned that she was interested in makeup, and we did our makeup together virtually. You all have these stories. You all will continue to have these stories.

It starts with the belief that there is enough time in the day for us to achieve what we believe is important. We must ask ourselves what those truly important things are and how we want to spend our time. We must be honest about our tendencies and what has worked well or not so well for us, and we must build our systems accordingly. We can change and adapt when we want to or have to—we've proven we can do it. It doesn't have to be a big, grand event. It can be accomplished in small moves.

Teacher Habits That Require Little Planning

As I previously mentioned, we educators often read books or attend professional learning and leave with this notion that we need to make big changes. Unsure about which steps to take to make those big changes, it's easy to shut down or criticize. I wonder what would happen, however, if we were to think about our classrooms in terms of habits, or small moves made over time. These kinds of moves require little planning on paper. Instead, they require us to plan how we will show up for others. For example, let's say you're concerned that students don't seem to be talking much when asked to work in groups. Instead of planning a big lesson or unit on interpersonal communication, what would happen if you were to make one small shift in your practice? While walking around the room, listen for smart things that kids say to their group. When you hear one, simply say, "What you are saying here is very important. Would you mind sharing that with the whole room when we come back together as a class?" That student is likely going to feel seen and heard. That student is likely going to feel important and like their contributions matter. The class is going to notice that you elevated that student's voice, and other students will want the opportunity to have their own voices amplified in the future. You didn't plan a full lesson on communication. You didn't plan an entire unit filled with new material. You didn't have to find anything online, and you didn't have to wait in line to make copies. You made a small tweak in your response to students. The more you do that small thing, adjusting and reflecting as necessary, the more outcomes will improve. It took little time for you to plan that move. Over time, it's a move you won't have to think about much—you'll just do it.

Or maybe that's not the move at all. Maybe you notice students are hesitant to speak to each other when working in groups, and your curiosity leads you to discover that they don't know each other's names. So, your small move involves building more classroom community so students know each other better. Whatever the move may be, doing it consistently and reflectively means it will take less effort over time. And suddenly you're making another new small move until that move becomes a habit too.

Let's say this goes on for an entire school year. You make a new move until each move becomes a habit. This takes two months or so each time. That's roughly 4.5 new habits over nine months. Let's say each habit encompasses 1 percent of your workday—that means you've gotten 4.5 percent better in one school year, and that's pretty good! Let's say that every person in your school makes the same commitment. That's big math right there! Suddenly, what was small is not so small. Small moves. Big impact. This is not to say that we should not go big with some of our efforts. What I'm saying is that our moves don't have to be big to make a positive impact, and for some of us, that feels much more accessible and attainable.

To this day, there are things I say and mean that I've practiced saying and meaning. They are small but impactful. To start, when someone thanks me for something, I often reply, "My pleasure." When I see someone in the hallway, after we exchange greetings, I often reply, "It's nice to see you." I've practiced saying these things so much that I mean them, and I mean them without expending much energy thinking about them. I also just feel good after I say these kinds of things, and saying these things seems to make others feel good too. I've also practiced not saying certain things—things that didn't leave me feeling so great. For example, when people would ask me how I was doing, I used to sometimes reply, "Living the dream." But we all know that when people say that it means the opposite, and that doesn't feel great. Instead of living the dream, we can build the dream one small step at a time, in ways that feel really good and manageable, in ways that make the lives of others better in the process too.

No Small Words or Actions in a School

My dad used to do little activities with me as a kid that I will never forget. He would ask me who was singing a song on the radio and get super excited when I got it right. He loved music. He would tell me,

"Don't worry. Be happy." To this day, it's important to me that I know the names of music artists. And when I'm in a worry spiral, I will repeat that mantra: "Don't worry. Be happy." The same holds true for the teachers in my life. They said and did little things that lifted me up in some cases and tore me down in others. Our words and actions matter in a big way. The small stuff is, in fact, the big stuff. I will never forget when my second-grade teacher told my mom that I would "always be a C student in math." In just one sentence, she wrecked my math confidence, which I'm still working to rebuild today.

When you're building habits as an educator, a meaningful place to start is your daily interactions with yourself and others. There are no small words or small actions in a school because you never know what battles your students and colleagues are facing. You are facing difficulties yourself. We all struggle. We will all have tough moments. One of the most important habits we can cultivate is mindfulness. We can simply pay attention to the body language of others in response to the environment, what we say, and what others say. And we must remember to be mindful of our own well-being and what we need to be OK too. We must take care of ourselves so we can take care of others.

The other day I volunteered to lead the conversation around a chapter in the book we were reading as a district cabinet team. In this book, like many leadership books, there was an emphasis on taking the time to celebrate the unique contributions of others. And honestly, I could have used a little encouragement myself at that moment. Sometimes, when I'm lacking in encouragement, encouraging others makes me feel better. So, I gave each member of the cabinet a handwritten note that explained something specific that I appreciated about their leadership. A few of them reached out to me after the fact, telling me they really appreciated my words and didn't realize how much they needed that affirmation. They were just brief notes, but this was a small move that seemed to really matter to them. This experience reminded me that while many leaders seem calm and unflappable, we are human beings with insecurities and struggles. Even staff and students who don't seem like they need appreciation and care can benefit from appreciation and care. The key is understanding that not everyone receives appreciation and care in the same way. We need to be open to caring for people in the ways they want to be cared for. Here's an example: birthdays. We often differ in how we want our birthdays to be or not be acknowledged. If I plan a surprise party for someone who hates surprise parties, they aren't going to feel celebrated in the way I'd hoped. If I knowingly plan a birthday event for someone who would like to spend a quiet evening at home, I've made someone else's celebration about my preferences instead of theirs. What matters is how we make others feel—not how we *intended* to make others feel.

Reflection Questions:

- What is a small habit you would like to cultivate for yourself personally or professionally?
- As a teacher or leader, can you think of a habit that requires little planning but when done with intentionality could have a positive impact on student learning?

CHAPTER 5

NOURISH THE BLOOMS

When a flower doesn't bloom, we fix the environment in which it grows, not the flower.

—ALEXANDER DEN HEIJER

In the introduction, I told you the story of how my dad died of leukemia when I was in the first grade. I shared the first question I asked my mom after receiving the news: "Will we have enough food to eat?" I also mentioned how difficult it was to return to school after such a traumatic loss and how grateful I am that Mrs. Boggess took such good care of me. That school year ended, as all school years do, but grief knows no limits. I had experienced an ACE: adverse childhood experience. So, in the years that followed, I struggled both emotionally and academically. Unfortunately, my second-grade teacher was not as empathetic as the first. She seemed to be all about rote academics, rules, and obedience. I was afraid of her and so were many of my classmates. My ability to think clearly and deeply was limited. The messy, chaotic inside of my desk reflected the inside of my heart and mind. One day, my second-grade teacher asked us to take out our scissors and glue to complete an assignment that involved construction paper. I cannot remember what the actual assignment was or why we were doing it, but I do remember being unable to find scissors and glue. After several minutes of searching, my teacher became irritated and sent me out into the hall with nothing but the worksheet and construction paper. She told me to "figure it out."

I felt hopeless. How was I going to make this happen? I didn't have scissors or glue. With big tears streaming down my face, I tried to fold and tear the construction paper and then licked it to see if I could get it to somehow stick to the worksheet. At that moment, a substitute teacher who also happened to live a few doors down from our house was walking by. She was aware of my dad's passing and the challenges facing my family. She looked concerned, and she kneeled down next to me and asked, "What's wrong?" I explained that I couldn't find my scissors or glue but that I had to find a way to complete this assignment. I could see that she was becoming quite angry with my teacher, especially given that she knew my personal circumstances. She left for a moment, came back, handed me some scissors and glue, and went off to report this matter to the principal.

What you do in your classroom and school matters. In a big way. We are always making an impact on students and colleagues, whether good or bad. Had my second-grade teacher taken more time to truly see me and all that I was battling that year, my learning experience could have looked quite different. Learning is not separate from lived experience. Learning is an integral part of lived experience. I am easily triggered when we use the well-intentioned phrase "preparing students for the real world." Losing a parent and worrying about whether you will have enough food to eat is about as real as it gets. What our students experience inside and outside of school is a part of their lives. Stories from inside and outside of the schoolhouse are the ones we tell around campfires and dinner tables. They are stories that shape us. So, when we speak as if what our students are experiencing in school or at home isn't "the real world," we are minimizing a big part of our students' daily lives. And we wonder why sometimes kids think school doesn't count or doesn't matter. We often treat school as if it's separate from reality. We often *do* school as if it's separate from reality too. Think about it. Many of the rules that we use to teach students responsibility come from this idea that we must be hard on kids so they can be tough enough to do life in the "real world." When we think and do school this way, we are treating students as empty vessels to be filled up with knowledge, dispositions, and attributes instead of human beings who bring their own talents and gifts—talents and gifts that we can leverage for the greater good in our ecosystems.

Nourishing Blooms

I was brave last year and bought some real plants for my office. One of those plants is a peace lily. My friend Lucrecer Braxton is a plant champion who graciously gave me guidance on how to keep this peace lily happy. She jokingly told me that peace lilies are dramatic and sassy. Among the many tips she shared, she told me that if my peace lily bloomed, I could cut those blooms if I wanted my lily to put energy into making more leaves instead. Otherwise, energy would go to the blooms.

This was helpful information, and it got me thinking about blooming in our schools. We cut the blooms a lot in education, and while that can be a great thing for plants, it's not so great for educators or students. What does blooming look like among staff members? Often, it looks like that place where nurtured talent and energy collide. It looks like people who are excited about and confident in their work. It looks like doing things that aren't required of us but that we want to do anyway. Things that light us up. Things that light kids up. Things that make other people feel seen, special, and connected. Blooming looks like bringing light in the darkness. Hope to those feeling hopeless.

We've all seen it. It's easy to spot someone who is in a state of flow. I love to facilitate meetings that inspire learning, nurture connection, and move change forward. Meetings where we get things done while having fun are my jam. I think about what Mary Poppins said: "In every job that must be done, there is an element of fun." When I facilitate meetings, I can feel that I'm enjoying the work and that others are too. People also tell me that I'm good at it. I'm not writing that to brag; I'm sharing it to illustrate that the things people say you're good at and that you really enjoy—that's where you're blooming. Those are your gifts and strengths. I recently facilitated a conversation about school with a group of high school students. It was a place for them to speak honestly about their experiences. Afterward, one of them told me, "I just felt really comfortable and safe and heard. It felt good." That's how you know. You feel it and others speak it.

It's inspiring to be around people who are expanding into their biggest and best selves. I remember the first time I had the opportunity to hear George Couros speak. I laughed. I cried. I was on the edge of my seat learning and didn't want it to ever end. I feel that way every time I hear him speak. Being around people who are nourishing their blooms and the blooms of others makes you want to be a better person. The best kind of people are the ones who are working on being their best while helping you be your best. That's George. What's even better is that he could easily stay focused on writing books and speaking to crowds. He's so talented as both an author and speaker. But he also goes out of his way to nourish the skills and talents of other educators, encouraging them and making them feel seen. He nudges people to dream a little bigger and try a little harder. He simply makes you feel like you are filled with limitless human potential.

That's what great teachers and leaders do. They use their skills and strengths to amplify the strengths of the group. Our school cultures are not separate from us. We are each responsible for building a positive school culture. Climate is how we feel at work. Culture is how we do our work. That's what is so wonderful about culture—it's an action verb. We do culture. Not one day, but every day. Every day we are either building a culture that makes people better or doesn't. When we focus on being our best selves while amplifying the strengths of others, we create what Shawn Achor would call a "super bounce" of positivity that can propel all of us into our greatest potential faster. As he explains in his book *Big Potential*, "When jumping on a trampoline, you can only jump so high. But if you can convince someone to jump next to you—and you time it right—their extra weight augments the potential energy, and in turn, you both spring up much higher. Big Potential is the super bounce that is possible only with others jumping next to you."[1] The work gets better when we work well together.

When we shine and genuinely encourage others to shine and when we lean on each other's unique gifts and talents, we all shine brighter together, and our schools and communities become better places to work and learn.

Often, teachers receive feedback that is heavily focused on areas where they already know they aren't as strong, which is deflating. Because of this, many teachers believe this kind of feedback is expected, and thus some do the same with students. Who wants to spend the day hearing about and working on areas where they already know they struggle? Sure, we need to be proficient at essential skills, but the world is much more likely to benefit if we all learn to maximize our strengths, work well together, and leverage the strengths of others.

Late Work & Writing Utensils

I find it interesting that there are hardworking teachers who struggle to get their grades turned in on time and yet don't accept late work from students. There are teachers who are five minutes late to staff meetings but have zero tolerance for student tardiness. Busy teachers show up to meetings and ask to borrow a pen but won't give students writing utensils because they need to learn responsibility. Things happen. That is life. Now, listen, I've been that teacher. I'm not writing this to bring guilt into anyone's heart—though I'm not trying to save you from that feeling either. I've felt it before, and I will feel it again about my practices. Often that feeling in your gut is a good thing. It's where change starts. You don't have to spend a lot of time there; just allow that feeling to carry you into reflection and perhaps a change in practice that feels right given new information. I'm merely asking us all to press pause and consider the rationale for much of what we do in schools.

Being human is hard. Growing up is hard. The world can be harsh. Perhaps instead of preparing our students for the hard realities of this world, we should instead equip them to create a kinder, gentler world—a better world. And perhaps the best way to do that is to make school even better than the world outside of school. That way, our students can see what's possible, and they'll understand the kind of world they want to create. We can teach students self-awareness strategies, communication, and collaboration skills. Equipped with durable skills, students can make a positive difference at any age. All learners deserve people who have their backs, who stand up for them and for what is right. All learners deserve people who see them, listen to them, celebrate them, and encourage them to lead with their strengths.

Utilizing Student Strengths in School

When I was a student, the best part of my day was often when the school day ended. I would go to dance class and practice for three to four hours, loving almost every minute of it. I was blooming at the dance studio. What got me out of bed and to school every day was the fact that my mom wouldn't allow me to go to dance class if I missed school. There are many students in our schools who feel the same way. The part of the day that makes them come alive is when the school day ends and extracurriculars begin. Sadly, there are also students who don't look forward to any part of their day. Many are spending most of their school day working on areas of deficit and feeling hopeless. They go from math class and ELA class into math remediation and ELA remediation. That's a lot of time spent working on areas of perceived deficit.

Don't get me wrong. Reading, writing, and mathematical thinking are critical skills. However, imagine spending your entire day at work on things that were hard for you and that you didn't like. Yikes. Something about that does not sound very motivating. How many of our learners know what they're good at? How many have time to enjoy being good at something during their day? How many learners get to spend time in a flow state each day? I love being in schools where learners use their strengths to be true contributors in the school environment. I love hearing kids on the morning announcements. I love when kids create school podcasts, design school or community event logos, write weekly updates and news articles. It's fun to see kids leading their own parent-teacher conferences and planning school events. It's a delight to see students helping the teacher establish learning norms and arranging the classroom during the first week of school.

We often wonder why kids don't feel the same kind of pride and ownership in their schools as the adults, yet we often limit their opportunity to contribute and build our school culture. I wonder what would happen if we were to nourish their blooms? What would happen if that same big energy we bring into remediating areas for growth was put into nourishing areas of bloom? We don't blame plants when they wilt. Instead, we look at the environment. Do they need more water? More sunlight? Or perhaps a little less? Instead of blaming learners for wilting in the conditions, we need to change the conditions.

Nourishing the blooms within learners does not need to be an add-on to classroom instruction. Small moves can have a big impact. Let students help you when you have a tech issue. Let them help each other. Host silent Socratic discussions in your classroom where students respond to each other and to what they're reading in writing. This allows students who might not always share out loud an opportunity to be heard. Encourage students to write about choice books and topics of personal interest. Invite students to show their thinking in a variety of formats—those who love to draw will shine. Those who love to write will shine. Those who love to rap will shine. When we pay attention to what lights up each of our students and we give them opportunities to learn in ways that utilize their strengths, learning becomes more interesting and engaging. There are countless other small moves teachers can make that cultivate a healthy environment for blooming. If we aren't sure where to start, we can simply ask our students.

Human Beings, Not Just Scholars

I recently had the honor and privilege of listening to a group of roughly thirty students from our high school speak about their classroom learning experiences. As they shared what had engaged and inspired them to learn more deeply, it was clear how much they valued teachers who spent time getting to know them as human beings, not just scholars. As one student so aptly put it, "We've got the academic part of school down. We need to work on the human part." Shew. Think about that. When I dug a bit deeper into their thinking, students explained how much they valued the opportunity to have good conversations with their teachers about a variety of topics and not just the content they were learning. This makes a lot of sense when you consider the growth and development of the adolescent brain. Our students are desperately trying to understand the world around them, their place in this world, and the impact they can make. So, inevitably, adults are interesting to teens. Adults are living independent lives, and many high school students can see themselves getting closer to living independently (at least their adults hope so). What I find interesting about that student's comment is that I'm not so sure we have the academics part of school down just yet. To get to deeper levels of learning, we must be human centered in all that we do, including academics. Being human means getting curious about the world and caring enough to try, alongside others, to solve really complex problems and make the world better. According to the American Institutes for Research, "The combination of (1) a deeper understanding of core academic content, (2) the ability to apply that understanding to novel problems and situations, and (3) the development of a range of competencies, including collaboration skills and self-management, is called deeper learning."[2] There is no deep learning without being deeply human.

In a piece for New Pedagogies for Deep Learning, Gardner et al. explain:

> Research is also showing that the adolescent's brain is wired to connect with others and contribute to society. When young people give back to others as they do in Deep Learning, they are using their energy to do good in the world and this changes their brains in terms of the way they think, act and interact with others. The Deep Learning experiences young people have builds up their neural pathways—the networks of connections. What they don't use, they lose. When kids are activated by the 6 Global Competencies, their brains develop very differently than students who are "sitting and getting" content that is irrelevant to their life.[3]

What they don't use, they lose. That really stood out to me. It actually reminds me of an argument in the gifted education world. (Now, I'm not here to start a gifted debate. I believe all people are gifted in something and sadly, many times those gifts are not amplified by traditional school.) But I've seen teachers roll their eyes at an adolescent's earlier gifted identification and explain, "That was in third grade." Presuming that a test was appropriately and ethically administered, a student can't be gifted accidentally or temporarily. But I do wonder what we're doing that makes kids less curious and less awake as they continue in school. What are we doing that is causing student thinking and caring muscles to atrophy?

Hope & Relationships in School

Hope is the belief that tomorrow will be different from today and that we have the power to make it so. For many of our students, every school day looks the same. And if our students are experiencing disconnection from each other and their teachers, they'll feel hopeless. That group of high school students I mentioned earlier all said the most critical factor for high levels of learning and engagement in the classroom is a relationship with the teacher. In her 2013 TED talk, "Every Kid Needs a Champion," Rita Pierson asserts, "Kids don't learn from people they don't like."[4] We tend to learn more from the teachers and administrators we believe like us. When we believe someone enjoys and values us, it creates a sense of emotional safety that is needed to open our hearts and minds to new learning.

Some learners are harder to like than others. Often those who need love the most ask for it in the most unlovable ways. So, we must find something we like about all learners. What we look for, we find. The student whose sense of humor and charisma prove distracting in class has the potential to be an influential leader when we channel those gifts for the betterment of the classroom community. The student who questions the fairness of our decisions has a strong sense of advocacy and can help us reflect and grow as long as we find constructive ways to dialogue. The student who asks many questions may be deeply curious or detail oriented, both attributes that can be leveraged in the classroom. Imagine this student previewing a lesson before you bring it to the entire class. I bet their questions could lead to tweaks that would make learning clearer and a smidge more engaging for students.

When we look for the good, we see the good, and when we see the good, we should celebrate it with genuine spirit and specificity so the person believes it. We can learn something from everyone, and every individual has something valuable to offer that can enhance learning and the school experience. I ran into a superintendent at a conference recently. Dr. Kimberly P. Miller was the principal at the middle school where I was a seventh-grade ELA teacher. She was someone who I always believed liked me and cared about me. As a principal, she invested her time, energy, and resources in my growth and development because she believed I could make a positive impact. It was clear she had high expectations, and I worked hard to reach those expectations. When I saw her at the conference, she said something along the lines of, "I am so proud of you. I always knew you were going to do great things, but you've exceeded what I imagined." I cried happy tears on my drive home. We are never too old or too experienced to appreciate genuine affirmation. It matters whether we appreciate the adults in our schools. Our students are watching. They watch to see how we treat each other. They watch to see if we say hello and offer an encouraging word. They listen when we speak in whispers to each other in the hallway. They watch how we talk about ourselves, each other, our students, and our world. Our students need hope for the future, and a great way to grow hope is through caring, healthy relationships.

According to Jamie Meade, vice president and chief of staff for Battelle for Kids, "Several academic studies indicate that hope is a more robust predictor of future success than a student's ACT score, their SAT score, and their GPA. In fact, hope is a greater predictor than GPA as to whether or not a college freshman will return to campus in the 2nd semester."[5] Hope is the belief that challenges are simply obstacles to be overcome and that we have the skills needed to overcome those obstacles to create the future we desire. There are many great strategies from BFK and other credible sources for growing hope in students. Jamie Meade explains that when students can't see potential in themselves and lack hope for the future, teachers can lend them their hope—but only when they themselves have hope to give.[6]

An effective way to take great care of students is to take really good care of educators. Relationships are not the only way to do this, but they can be foundational to success. And taking great care of educators is not just an endeavor for administrators. It's the work of all of us.

Empathizing with the Experience of Others

I'm not saying we need to be besties with every colleague. I'm also not saying we must be fond of people who are unkind or unsafe. Generally speaking, there is good in every human being, and the sooner we find it and celebrate it, the sooner people will be inspired to bloom into their greatest potential. It's often the good that grows us, not the bad. Long gone is the negative feedback sandwich. You know, the one where you start with a positive, give constructive criticism in the middle, and then end on a positive note. Many of us have gotten that feedback sandwich, and many of us have focused solely on the negative, casting the positives aside. I'm most motivated when I see that I'm making progress in areas where I excel. This doesn't mean that we should never give difficult feedback or feedforward. It means that we should be thoughtful about how much and how often.

I'm ashamed to admit that as a young high school English teacher, I marked up everything that was wrong on papers. Capitalization, spelling, comma splices (if you don't know what a comma splice is, that's a fun one, look it up). I marked up grammar and punctuation and content too. It took me a long time to grade each paper, but I thought, "They will know that I read every word." I did my grading in purple because I'd learned somewhere that purple was less scary than red, which can make us think of blood and danger.

It turns out it doesn't matter what color you use. If you are determined to point out everything that's wrong, everything feels wrong.

There are so many issues with this approach. To start, the person doing the learning was me—because I made all the corrections. But more importantly, I can only imagine how my students felt going home with those papers. To my former students, I'm so sorry. I thought I was helping, but I can see now that I was hurting. I was more focused on showing you that I read your paper than on how you received my comments. I'm sorry for how that made you feel. I can see now how much more inspiring it would have been to amplify the good and to be very choosy about areas for growth.

I recently went to a new dentist, and it was a surprisingly delightful experience. The dentist and hygienist asked me about my goals for the visit and took time to listen. Isn't that interesting? Have you ever thought about going into a dental appointment with goals instead of just a prayer that you don't have a cavity or a desire for the satisfaction of professionally cleaned teeth? I thought about it and told them I clench my teeth at night and that I've been told I have gum inflammation despite flossing every day. Did we still clean my teeth and check for cavities? Sure. But while they were doing the cleaning, they kept my goals in mind, and they conferenced with me at the end regarding them. This made my visit feel a little less like something done to me and more like a collaborative dialogue. Sometimes, school feels like something done to our students—but when we listen and make even just a little space for their specific areas of interest and concern, it can spark energy for learning. You can do this in small ways, like leaving one row on a rubric blank for things that really matter to a student. It can be incredibly empowering for students to determine what they want you to notice in their work and how they want you to measure their success in that key area.

Educating minds is our work as educators. We are in the brain business. Our minds, however, do not live in isolation from our emotions. So, a big part of our work is to give learners a sense of safety so they can spend less energy on worrying and more energy on learning.

A great way to signal to adults and students alike that they can relax and enjoy learning is through celebrating their individual brilliance and contributions.

Again, this doesn't have to be a grand gesture. Don't underestimate the impact a small, honest, and kind word can have on another person and their well-being. Whether you're delivering a handwritten note, sharing a positive thought about a person's work out loud, sending an email or text, making a phone call, or writing a post on social media—every word matters. A thoughtful word, eye contact, a smile, or simply sitting with others in their pain can do wonders. We can fill others with hope and possibility so they can bloom into their best selves and achieve more than they ever dreamed possible. We can do so in small acts performed consistently over time with a genuine heart and spirit. We have that kind of power as educators. We have that kind of power as human beings. And this means withholding kind words or sharing unkind ones can also have great impact.

Our school district recently started a teacher academy. Juniors and seniors take classes to learn more about school-based professions and effective pedagogy, and then seniors also have the opportunity to participate in internships for two to four class periods a day. These internships take place in our elementary schools and middle school. It's a wonderful experience for both our high school students and the students they support. Our elementary and middle school teachers are also grateful for the help.

The program happens to be located next to our professional meeting space, which is nestled in our high school. It dawned on me that there are many ways we can partner with this program, especially given its proximity to us.

Every week our district administrators, principals, associate principals, and coaches go on instructional rounds. We leave encouraging notes for the teachers we visit. After we exit each classroom, we also fill out a form about what we saw. The form does not include teacher names but does capture the content and grade level. These walks have many purposes. We review our purpose each week so we don't lose sight of our intentions.

The purpose of our learning walks is to:

- Provide specific, positive feedback to teachers
- Practice uncovering effective instructional practices and strengthen our collective capacity to engage in meaningful dialogue with each other and with teachers about instruction
- Gather data to inform professional learning needs

One week we decided to invite students from the teacher academy to come along. Seven seniors joined us around the table. We gathered before going into classrooms to get to know each a bit better but to also help students understand our purpose for these walks.

The seniors joined us in visiting ninth-grade classes. The administrators/instructional coaches wrote quick notes while we were in the rooms, and when the four of us stepped out into the hall together, the two seniors in the group paired up to work on their own notes. The administrator/instructional coach pairing completed the form, which we keep as a shortcut on our phones.

When we gathered after this experience, our students' observations blew us away. Their thoughts about classroom environment and effective pedagogy were deeply insightful. It's amazing how knowledgeable they became in just a few short months in the teacher academy. Additionally, their professionalism was top tier. We explained our norms to them, including not using people's names if you have something critical to say about what you saw in the classroom. They honored and upheld our norms in such a beautiful, human-centered manner.

An unintended consequence of this experience was their heightened respect for the hard work and intentionality teachers pour into their lessons. Our students explained that more goes into lesson planning than they realized; they said they have deeper respect for their teachers now. Some of them said they thought all students should have this experience. They also saw the value of positive feedback to encourage teacher growth and learning. Finally, because they were in teaching internships, they left with ideas they wanted to try with the students they served.

There is a lot we can learn from this. To start, trust students. We were a little nervous about how this would go, but this was the most encouraging and rich dialogue we've had to date in our instructional rounds. Sitting at a table with students changes the conversation in the best possible way because they are living the experiences we are working to create for them. Their feedback (or feedforward) is paramount.

We also learned the value of students empathizing with the teacher experience. I'm a big believer in shadowing students because it helps adults empathize with the student experience. However, I had not considered how powerful it would be to have students doing the same. When we all have an opportunity to meaningfully understand each other and our roles within the school, care and connection increase. When our understanding and sense of community increase, meaningful learning is more likely to occur.

Utilizing Staff Strengths in School

Asset-based feedback (or feedforward) matters just as much for staff as it does for students. But even positive feedback isn't always easy to hear at first. Some teachers shut their doors and keep their magic to themselves because they don't want other teachers to feel bad or like they need to change. Others hide their blooms because they don't want other people to think they're showing off. Some blooming staff members get uncomfortable when the principal gives them a shout-out because they don't want to look like the favorite. It's hard to talk about, but we've all seen it.

When I was an assistant principal in a middle school, I started sending weekly shout-outs to staff. I was new, and I thought this would be a great way to contribute to a positive school culture. I kept a list of staff members' names so I could keep track of who had received a shout-out and who I needed to celebrate in future weeks. Some teachers said this made them feel embarrassed. They didn't want other staff members to give them a hard time about it.

If you catch yourself judging an educator who is doing something awesome for kids, take a moment before doing anything with that feeling. Identify where that feeling may be coming from. Perhaps you're feeling inadequate. Perhaps you feel underappreciated or underutilized. Perhaps you wish you had the confidence to try something new. Whatever the reason, find a way to work through it without bringing a bloomer down. Go out of your way to encourage that brave bloomer. The work goes better when we all have a chance to bloom. When someone shines brightly, it doesn't take any light away from you. There is enough light for all of us, and the brighter we shine, the more clearly we can find our way through the darkness together. Life is hard. We don't need to make it any harder by bringing other people down. We are responsible for every child in our school, not just the ones in our classroom. So, when you champion another teacher and make them feel like they can bloom into their best teacher self, you are having a positive impact on more kids. And isn't that what we all went into education to do?

Relationships Outside of School

While educators bring many strengths to schools, they can ultimately only do so much—each educator is one person with a specific set of knowledge and skills that they're growing. We cannot know it all, we shouldn't be expected to know it all, and we shouldn't have to do it all alone. This is why it's important for schools to grow students' networks outside of school. In fact, as Julia Freeland Fisher writes on the website Education Next, growing these networks is key to shrinking the achievement gap: "Employers consider the importance of 'real-world' relevance in education, but schools fail to pursue instructional models that could connect authentically what happens inside classrooms with the wide range of industries in the real world."[7] Raising the future workforce and raising good community members is not strictly the responsibility of educators; it's the responsibility of everyone.

Our students need access to people and experiences beyond those that school and home can provide. It is imperative that we begin growing our students' networks and give them exposure to opportunities and experiences that deepen their understanding of the world, themselves, and the future they want to create.

For example, an effective way for students to learn about space exploration might be to connect with people who work in the space industry. When a teacher preps the class for a virtual call with a space engineer, that's an incredible learning experience. This kind of virtual Q&A approach is a great place to start. But beyond that, it's critical that we create opportunities for our students to engage with local community partners in small group conversations, working on and learning about challenges in various industries and communities. This can help them understand all the possibilities for their future. For example, let's look at the medical industry. When students go to the doctor, they'll usually see the person working the front desk, the nurse, and the doctor. However, they don't see the business or finance professionals, the manufacturers, or the people who provide training on technology and medicine. Suddenly, there are so many more jobs to consider in the medical industry.

The more students learn and experience beyond school walls, the clearer they become about what interests them, how they want to positively impact their communities, and what lifestyle they desire. We can support this reflection by asking students questions. What problems do you want to solve? Which problems interest you less? Which work environments feel right for you? Which ones don't? Exposure to a variety of people, industries, and learning experiences can lead to a stronger understanding of self. Feeling like you have many options and possibilities is a hope-giving experience. When students have a more robust network and a stronger understanding of how others have overcome obstacles, suddenly what didn't feel possible feels possible.

Rebecca Elliott, a high school English teacher, told me about how she wanted to give students in her storytelling class the opportunity to experience stories outside of the school walls. Adults lead busy lives, so it can be hard to find someone willing to take the time to dialogue with students. But there is a subset of our population that is not only willing to share stories but also often available: members of senior living communities. Ms. Elliott took her class down the street to a local senior living community. The students enjoyed listening to the stories, the senior citizens enjoyed telling their stories, and they also enjoyed asking the students about themselves. It was clear that some of the students relished that undivided, kind attention from an adult. Ms. Elliott said that students went into the experience afraid these adults would be mean to them or talk down to them. Similarly, some of the senior citizens had preconceived notions about "kids these days" and were surprised by how well the students carried themselves and engaged in the conversation. Through those conversations about life and work experiences, students discovered a world of possibilities while simultaneously learning how to tell great stories—a skill that is often overlooked. The better we become at telling the inspiring stories of our schools, classrooms, and students, the more knowledgeable our communities become and the more hope floats.

Growing student networks is not only important in closing opportunity gaps; it's a necessary step toward changing the way people view our school systems. We all need each other. Schools need support from their communities, communities need support from their schools, and students need support from all of us. We bloom when we work together.

Reflection Questions:

- Who is a super bloomer in your ecosystem? How might you give them the energy they need to keep growing bigger and brighter than they ever thought possible?

- Who is someone who makes you feel like you can bloom into your biggest and most beautiful self? Have you told them? How might you get more time with them?

- What small moves can you make to amplify the strengths of learners in your classroom and school?

- How might you make small moves to celebrate your colleagues and students?

- How might you invite students to share more feedback with you about their classroom or school experience?

- How might you make learning more relevant and connected to the community? How might you give students opportunities to grow their network and experiences beyond the school walls?

CHAPTER 6

POPSICLES AND CONGA LINES

People have to take chances in order to do something extraordinary.

—PRIYA PARKER

In his book *Be Great*, Dwight Carter writes, "Nearly every meaningful experience in life boils down to the relationship you have with others."[1] But what does building strong relationships look like? It's not magic—and it's not simply handwritten notes. It's genuine care. In a world that moves so quickly and is filled with distractions, it's the people who choose to make smaller moments feel special who capture our hearts and attention.

Have you ever spent time with someone who looked you in your eyes and seemed genuinely interested and curious about you and what you had to say? You know, the kind of conversations where time and space seem to matter less because you are both just savoring the present moment. Will Guidara is the former co-owner of Eleven Madison Park. Under his leadership, this New York restaurant was named number one on the World's 50 Best Restaurants list in 2017. Known for his excellence and leadership in customer service, Guidara describes savoring moments with others in his book, *Unreasonable Hospitality: The Remarkable Power of Giving People More Than They Expect*: "I often describe 'being present' as caring so much about what you're doing that you stop caring about everything you need to do next."[2] It's what our classrooms and schools need: just a little more focus on being in the moment and a little less focus on the other noise. Easier said than done, right? Easier said than done when you aren't the one controlling what gets added to your plate as a teacher? Yep. But many of these impactful moves are small, require little to no planning, and can make an immense difference when executed consistently with intentionality and care.

Greetings & Conversations

There are students and staff who go entire school days without hearing their names. Knowing and using names correctly is a small move that can have a profound impact on people. When people look us in our eyes and use our names correctly, we are more likely feel seen and like we belong. We feel it would have mattered if we hadn't come to school or work that day because we would have been missed. I love to see teachers standing at their doors during class exchange, greeting students by name and asking them questions about themselves. I love seeing administrators and instructional coaches model this during staff meetings and professional learning days. Greeting students at the door is not a profound move, but it's one that requires intentionality and discipline. It requires committing to that practice even on the days when we don't feel like it. In "Welcoming Students with a Smile," educational researcher Youki Terada shares that recent studies indicate greeting students at the door increases student engagement by 20 percent. It also decreases disruptive behavior by 9 percent. Terada explains, "Spending a few moments welcoming students promotes a sense of belonging, giving them social and emotional support that helps them feel invested in the learning."[3] Quite simply, relationship moves such as greeting students at the door make meaningful learning more accessible for students.

Livia Chan, head teacher, author, and presenter, told me about how she takes this a step further by having her students sit and face each other, address each other by name, and connect in conversation. She says this allows them to see each other's hearts more clearly. Isn't that beautiful? The idea that we can see each other's hearts more clearly if we face each other? What I also love is that it matters whether the teacher knows each student's name *and* it matters whether students know each other's names. Think of how much more seen and valued we all feel when everyone is focused on caring for our community. Dr. Tim Kubik, cofounder of Project ARC, said it best when leading a professional learning day that I was privileged to be part of: "Perhaps all we need is each other. Really each other."

That sense of being both seen and held can do powerful things for learning in the classroom. Dr. Mary Hemphill, a K–12 educator, leadership coach, author, and public speaker, describes this further in her chapter in the book *Because of a Teacher*: "Understanding that students are transitioning from home where they have routines, strategies for self-care, and a comfortable communication system allows educators to determine how to develop some of these components in their classrooms. Although the environment may be different, the need is the same: students seek safety. It's human nature."[4] It is vital that learners feel comfortable in our schools and like they can not only be themselves but are appreciated for being themselves. As Dr. Hemphill states, routines, strategies for self-care, and a comfortable communication system are three factors that can play an important role in building that sense of safety. There will likely be variations in how this looks for every student, which is why it's important that we know each learner in meaningful ways. Peers and the classroom community also play a key role in developing these components that are critical to ensuring we can grow as learners and human beings.

Design for Engagement

There's a meme that says something to this effect: "If I die, I hope it's during a staff meeting because the transition to death would be so subtle." So relatable. And there are students in our classrooms who also feel this disengaged.

I've been to far too many meetings and professional learning experiences where the presenter ironically talks *at* the group about student engagement and effective instructional practices. It's no wonder that when administrators visit classrooms, teachers often feel nervous if they aren't presenting information or talking in front of the class. It's not because teachers think that is good teaching (at least not most of the time). It's because many teachers think that's what administrators think is good teaching. This is because that's the instructional style in many team and staff meetings.

Teachers often receive evaluative feedback about the amount of teacher talk versus student talk in the classroom. This is because the person doing the most talking tends to be the person doing the most thinking and learning. The same is true in adult learning spaces. If administrator talk outweighs teacher talk, then it's not really a meeting for teachers and teacher learning. Whether we are a teacher in the classroom or an administrator facilitating a team meeting, it's important to ensure equity of voice—to invite and make space for all participants to share and contribute. Too often in our meetings, one or two voices take up the most space in the room. The same is sometimes true in the classroom.

Listening for this as facilitators of adult and student learning is critical. I saw a post on social media by Adam Grant where he noted, "We pay too much attention to the most confident voices—and too little attention to the most thoughtful ones. Certainty is not a sign of credibility. Speaking assertively is not a substitute for thinking deeply. It's better to learn from complex thinkers than smooth talkers."[5] We must ensure that all of our learners are not only learning but contributing at a high level. For example, there are few things both easier and more powerful than a good turn and talk in the classroom (some call it a turn and learn). Essentially learners are invited to dialogue and briefly share their learning with someone seated near them. Such a practice requires little to no planning, can be executed quickly, and allows learners to process information in ways that feel can less intimidating than a whole-class discussion or even small-group dialogue. Plus learning can travel more quickly through a room when there are more voices engaged in the dialogue.

Another creative way to get learners actively participating in dialogue with their peers is to have them stand for the conversation. This helps them to step away from distractions on technology and the temptation of multitasking, a pervasive habit that I continue to struggle with. It's a simple but effective strategy I recently discovered in Peter Liljedahl's *Building Thinking Classrooms in Mathematics*. Please don't be dissuaded by the title of the book. I've found, as have many of the teachers I am honored to support, that many of the strategies mentioned in this text are effective across content and grade levels. Something about standing and brainstorming together on a whiteboard allows people to be more present for the conversation, and it also keeps the energy high. For those who may feel a bit intimidated by sitting across from someone when working on something challenging, the joy of working or thinking side by side takes the edge off and makes conversation feel more relaxed and natural. This is why many prefer to walk and talk. I find that if there's something weighing on me or that might feel heavy for the other person in the conversation, it's nice to talk about it while we're both moving in the same direction on a walk. That sensation of moving together makes me feel like we're in it together even if we may have differing views on the topic at hand. Liljedahl describes the impact of standing and working side by side: "In the 15 years that I have been engaged in the thinking classroom research, nothing we have tried has had such a positive and profound effect on student thinking as having them work in random groups at vertical whiteboards."[6] Many teachers use whiteboards because they can be a visual reminder that this is not permanent and we are just figuring it out together. Some of us may not have access to enough vertical whiteboards, in which case writing on windows with dry-erase markers or on large paper could work. Again, as I mentioned in the previous chapters, we don't want not being able to do something perfectly to prevent us from doing impactful work.

You may be thinking, "You started the chapter by telling us about looking each other in the eye and facing each other for the conversation, and now you're telling us to have students stand side by side when working." I think what we hope to achieve throughout a lesson together matters, and you can decide what works best in which instances for the learners you serve. For example, you will likely want students to turn and face each other when they're having a meaningful conversation about their perspectives and what they're thinking. And then, when it's time to solve something complex together, you may want them to stand side by side while they work out various solutions and agree upon a final answer.

I found what Liljedahl had to say about random groupings interesting. Often, we either allow students to choose their own groups or we choose groups for them. What Liljedahl explains made me want to try shaking up groups more often: "When teachers allow students to self-select, what we see is often a reflection of the social structures easily observable in the hallways. Students choose their friends, their affinity groups, or their social groups. These social structures can create barriers to collaboration in the classroom. With visibly random groupings, these barriers begin to fall away."[7] Creating random groupings in front of learners has the power to remove barriers to collaboration in the classroom or during professional learning. However, the number of students in the group matters significantly as well. According to Liljedahl, "We also learned that, from Grade 3 up, the optimal group size was three. . . . This is because for a group to be generative, it needs to have both redundancy and diversity (Davis & Simmt, 2003). Redundancy, in this context, reflects things that a group of students has in common—language, interests, experiences, knowledge. Without these commonalities they cannot even begin to collaborate. But if all they have is redundancy, they will not achieve anything beyond what they enter the group with. To be generative, they also need diversity; the things that individual members of the group bring that are not shared by the others—different ideas, viewpoints, perspectives, representations, et cetera. . . . For Grades K–2, however, the optional group size was two. Despite the lack of diversity this affords, students at this age are still developmentally in a stage of parallel play, and collaboration consists mostly of polite turn taking."[8]

Admittedly, as a secondary teacher, I often either moved students into pairs or into groups of four. I actually don't know why except that even numbers felt nice to me, ha. This has me thinking about the impact of simply placing students in grade three or higher (or even adult learners) into groups of three randomly, in front of learners, so they can see that it was a truly randomized grouping without any preconceptions on the teacher's part. Mike Ross, an instructional coach who often refers to himself as an instructional partner, likes to use a deck of cards to randomize groups in the classroom. He once explained to me, "One card goes on the table and the other three get handed out when students walk into the classroom." This strategy is effective because the groups are being randomized right in front of students, plus it allows the teacher to interact with students and greet them as they arrive. Additionally, this saves precious instructional minutes because groups are created before the lesson officially starts.

I incorporate learning in a similar fashion when I'm leading monthly meetings with administrators and instructional coaches. It is vital that our leaders continue to learn and grow. Often, for these learning segments, I print excerpts of readings on different colors of paper. After reading and perhaps considering a probing question, I ask colleagues to stand and find people with different colors of paper than theirs. I ask them to remain standing while they dialogue for a few minutes. I find that sometimes people take more ownership of their contributions to the conversation when they aren't reading or working on the same thing as the other people in their group. It's amazing how rich a conversation can be when people read different portions of an article or watch different short videos on the same topic. Some call this a jigsaw activity because you're putting together different readings and drawing conclusions as a group, much like someone putting together a puzzle. Upon closing the learning segment, I explain why I did this and remind colleagues that they weren't looking at their computers or phones while they were standing and conversing.

Standing, using vertical surfaces, and using randomized groups are powerful strategies for increasing learning engagement, which makes learning more accessible. We can also have different groups interact with each other during the learning activity, growing more ideas and thoughts throughout the classroom. I often enjoy sending one member of a group to visit another group to steal a thought or idea, or I will invite groups to walk around the room to look at other people's work. It's fun to see learners react to similarities and differences between their work and their approach, and it encourages the classroom community to value each other's voices and contributions. Perhaps most importantly, it gives learners an opportunity to expand their thinking and improve their work during the learning process, making learning less about what we alone can do and more about what we together can achieve.

It's worth mentioning that not everyone is comfortable with or learns best from group dialogue or conversation in general. Some groups or classroom settings may feel safer to learners than others. Let's remember what Dr. Hemphill calls a comfortable communication system. It's important that students can communicate with teachers and their peers in ways that work best for them. To understand what works best for each individual, we must build trust through nurturing relationships. We are more inclined to take risks and put ourselves out there (in collaborative groups, for example) when trust is intact. And there are plenty of ways for people to engage with learning and with others that do not involve talking in groups. If we solely rely on this methodology, we risk overstimulating learners who need a more serene learning environment. One example of interactive learning that does not involve conversation is a silent discussion. Simply writing a question or a quote and then having students respond to that and to each other in writing can be impactful. This can be done on vertical surfaces where the teacher can see the thinking and responses shared while they move throughout the room.

From Thrill and Delight to Gathering and Deciding

I love to feed people at meetings. I imagine this might sound silly or expensive, but it brings me immense happiness when I have an opportunity to thrill and delight people. When I get excited for the experience I'm creating in a meeting, other people get excited. While some researchers disagree, and I'm no expert, I believe that is emotional contagion in action again. I love greeting people at the door and putting candy on the tables. I love walking around with my snack basket, offering sweet and salty treats to hit the spot after a long day of teaching. Tiffany Brennan, a middle school principal, will take personal fountain drink orders from staff and put those orders on a cart with a salty or sweet snack to go with them. When we worked together, we would put some music on my portable speaker and roam the halls delivering these treats during teacher workdays. I couldn't help but dance to the music, and many teachers joined me. We enjoyed a little laugh about how goofy we looked too. Music has a way of changing the way a room, meeting, and interaction feels. It's nice to have a little fun at work. Why not? If we're going to be here, we may as well enjoy ourselves. You know?

Educational consultant and thought leader Katrice Quitter surveys participants before they join professional learning experiences. Among various questions she asks to ensure she honors each individual's unique identity and learning needs, she also asks people for their "walk-up song"—basically, what is the song that puts them in a good mood and gets them excited to do their best work and thinking? It's fun to see people hear their song playing and to see others try to guess which person picked the song. It's a great way to build connection and community while also making others feel seen.

But as great as songs and snacks can be, we need much more when we gather. To start, we need a compelling reason to gather beyond "we have to do this meeting every month" or "we have to go to class every day." We all need a meaningful purpose, a reason to care and show up, a reason beyond letter grades and paychecks. Certainly, those get many people in the door, but the energy is different when we've internalized a purpose for gathering. Educational leader and coach Kristi Otten has been reminding teachers of the purpose of their meetings since she saw a social media post by Adam Grant explaining that there are four reasons to meet: to decide, learn, bond, and do. Grant explains, "If it doesn't serve one of those purposes, cancel it."[9]

The clearer we are on why we're meeting, the better we can plan around those four main purposes. Sometimes, we're gathering for several purposes at once. As Priya Parker explains in *The Art of Gathering: How We Meet and Why It Matters*, "Reverse engineer an outcome: Think of what you want to be different because you gathered, and work backward from that outcome."[10] How do you want staff or students to feel when they leave? What do you want them to know and be able to do because of your time together? From there, you create the experience. I was recently working on a draft of an instructional framework with educational leader Ellie Preston. At the top of the document, she wanted us to outline in three simple sentences what we wanted teachers to know, how we hoped teachers would feel, and what we wanted to equip teachers to do. Such a simple yet impactful way to ensure you've defined your intended outcomes in advance whether it's for a meeting, a lesson, or an outline of information to be shared. Angela Faulhaber, a coach, educator, and dreamer, helped me brainstorm examples of how to design for the purpose of a meeting or lesson.

PURPOSE OF MEETING	MEETING SEGMENT EXAMPLE	LESSON SEGMENT EXAMPLE
BOND	**CHECK-IN AND CHECK-OUT** In one word, how are you feeling walking into or out of this meeting today?	**QUIZ-QUIZ-TRADE** Students use index cards to answer a question about themselves. At the teacher's signal, students move around the space, sharing information on the index card, trading it, then talking with other students.
LEARN	**JIGSAW READ** Find people in the room who read an excerpt or article on a different color paper than you, form a group of preferably three, and dialogue about connections you made.	**MENTOR TEXT MINGLE** Students choose a mentor text to read. As they read, students create a list of characteristics of the genre, then find two people in the room who read a different mentor text and compare notes.
DO	**PROFESSIONAL LEARNING DAY PRESENTERS** List the names of teachers you want to invite to facilitate a learning session at a professional learning day. Send them an invitation and tell them why you asked them specifically.	**POST-IT FEEDBACK** Give each student three Post-It notes to use to give feedback on a fellow student's work. Students take a gallery walk and write feedback on Post-Its, leaving them at their classmate's desk.
DECIDE	**SEMESTER VERSUS QUARTER GRADES** After eliciting feedback from multiple stakeholders, we meet to decide whether we will be issuing grades on a quarterly or semester basis according to what we believe is best for student learning.	**BOOK (PRODUCT) TASTING** Give students a chance to "taste" a variety of novels, primary source documents, articles, etc. Then create a way for students to decide where they want to spend their time — a Google form, or even a Post-It note with the students' top three choices.

"Deciding" meetings can be the most tricky and complex of them all, especially if you're trying to reach consensus with a group of students or staff. Consensus isn't always needed, but it can be very important, especially when you want to ensure that every member of the group truly has a voice and a say in something they'll play a critical role in executing. For example, defining priority standards (which I mentioned previously) may be a good time for a consensus protocol. This is because the prioritization of standards impacts how long we, as a community of practice, will spend on various types of learning in our classes. It can be helpful to execute a consensus protocol to support the group in determining whether they are fully committed to the decision or whether more conversation is needed.

I modified the 1–5 protocol from *The Art of Coaching Teams* by Elena Aguilar. In the book, she describes her Fist to Five Decision Making protocol.[11] Basically, once you think you have a decision, make sure everyone knows what it is and have them sign their name to their level of consensus. As long as everyone is a 3, 4, or 5, you can move forward. If anyone is a 1 or a 2, you keep talking until you can work it out. You can ask, "What would move this to a 3 for you?" Then, if there seems to be energy around a new decision, you rerun the protocol. But sometimes a person will come around to a 3 on the original decision. It is important to be clear in advance about what each level of consensus means and how we will respond to lower levels of consensus. This allows people to think critically about whether they are truly a 1 or 2 or could go with a 3. Having everyone put their name down ensures each person's voice is accounted for. If some members of the group are more comfortable sharing their thoughts 1:1 or feel uncertain about the level of psychological safety in the room, you might consider having everyone share their level of consensus and rationale for their response in writing with you privately. You know what will work best for the learners you serve and the topic at hand.

CONSENSUS PROTOCOL

DECISION ➤ **IMPLEMENT THE PROPOSED PRIORITY STANDARDS**

1. I am strongly opposed to this and need to see some big changes to approve it.
- Kristopher Mejia
- Angie Hines

2. I have serious reservations but could accept it with some changes.
- Salvador McClure
- Malachi Khan

3. I have reservations about this, but I could accept it without further discussion.
- Dante Richardson
- Xavier Sheppard
- Viviana Davis

4. I think it's a good idea, and I can live with it.
- Aspen McDonald
- Mabel Vo
- Theo Flowers
- Margot Cortez

5. I am in total agreement with this proposal.
- Tristen Costa
- Veda Fields
- Maggie Hawkins

This process is not always comfortable, but it's helpful when it's time to decide and commit. We've all been in meetings where it felt like we would never make a final decision and get to the action. This is one strategy for moving work forward, but it needs to be handled with care. As Elena Aguilar explains, "Common challenges with consensus include some group members showing reluctance to support a particular decision. Although it might be tempting to pressure dissenters to give in, don't do it. Dissenters often have an important idea that's been overlooked by the group. First acknowledge and accept their dissent, allow them to express their concerns in concrete terms, and then ask them to propose solutions to the issues they've raised."[12] As mentioned in previous chapters, people are more likely to support the work when they were a part of building it. Consensus protocols are one strategy, when appropriate, for ensuring that more voices have been involved in decisions.

At the start of the school year, in preparation for meetings and to take good care of people, I ask teammates to fill out a brief survey. Walk-up songs are part of it because I like to create playlists for our meetings with everyone's song, but I also ask other questions. I ask for addresses in case I want to send someone flowers or a little gift. I ask about snack preferences and favorite sweet treats. I ask about favorite restaurants, how people like to receive feedback, and about something they would do if they knew they couldn't fail.

I ask that last question because I like to know how I might champion big dreams and goals for the people I support. Whether we lead students or teachers, a big part of our job is removing barriers so people can do their best work and make progress toward ambitions and dreams. At minimum, simply asking people questions about what interests them and keeping the momentum going by taking interest in their aspirations is a great way to not only grow a relationship but support others in keeping their goals at the forefront of their minds. It's even better if we can make connections between what someone is working on and how the skills they're honing will bring them one step closer to their goals. Plus, you can be a connector. If you know people who share the same passion, connect those individuals. Help people of all ages grow their network. Be the person who says someone's name when they aren't present but there's an opportunity for them. This kind of goodwill will always come back to you tenfold. Grow your community by connecting people you love with people who love what they love.

Speaking of people we love, I also ask people to provide the contact information for someone they want to make proud. That last idea came from superintendent Natasha Adams during her time as a curriculum director. She asked us this question, and one year around the holidays, she asked the people we'd identified to write letters to us about why they were proud of us. She did this for the entire curriculum team, administrative assistants and all, and we were all crying our eyes out when our letters were handed to us. We each read specific lines aloud for the group. It was such a powerful moment. I've also seen principals walk around the school taking pictures of staff working with students so they can print and frame those images as gifts. Bob Buck, an educational leader and former elementary principal, sent pictures of each staff member in action to their families over the holidays with a note thanking them for "sharing them with us." As a parent or caregiver, can you imagine if your child's teacher sent you a picture of them working in the classroom with a note expressing what they love about your child, thanking you for "sharing them with us?" That is pure magic. What if it was a picture of your child smiling and playing? How fun! I'm smiling just thinking about it.

Whether it's music, snacks, handwritten notes, or simply being fully present with others, taking really good care of educators helps educators take really good care of students. In fact, we made that our brand as a secondary teaching and learning team. Too often we overlook the adults who serve kids in schools, or we use an either/or mindset: what's best for kids versus what's best for staff. You can focus on both, and both are needed to center the humanity of everyone and make a lasting impact on learning in schools. Well-cared-for people are more equipped to care for people. Well-cared-for students are more equipped to care for their classmates.

As I've said, it's not all about snacks and music and notes—all of that is nice, but it bears mentioning that if you don't take the time to genuinely listen, care, and acknowledge people, this stuff will come off as inauthentic, like a performance that's about you feeling good and not about what others truly need. It is important to care for others in the ways they individually want to receive care. With that caveat, in the hustle and bustle of daily life, thrill and delight need to be somewhat easy and convenient. So, we keep a speaker, snacks, and blank notes stored in the cabinets of our professional learning center, and we pull them out as needed. As a teacher, you could do the same. For example, maybe you want to have music playing between class periods. Let's say there's a student who always gets to class before the others. Perhaps you could have them put on the music so you can spend those precious minutes in the hallway greeting students. It doesn't need to be music, and maybe it can't be snacks, but you will decide what your special something will be. Perhaps it's simply the art of listening and following up.

I was recently talking with a friend who was amazed by the care her daughter's third-grade teacher showed. My friend explained that during the parent-teacher conference, she described for the teacher how her daughter feels when she knows she's going to be called on to read aloud to the class. Her daughter had said, "It makes me feel hot and upsets my belly." The teacher thanked my friend for sharing this information because her daughter's reaction had not been apparent. She asked questions about how they should proceed in the future. While my friend didn't want the teacher to change her instructional practices, the teacher's openness to doing so made her feel heard, understood, and like a true partner in her child's education.

Sometimes, we aren't able to agree upon solutions. However, there are ways to ensure that people still leave conversations feeling heard and understood. Some of my most uncomfortable conversations, where emotions were running high on the other side of the table or phone, have ended in people feeling heard and understood. Even when we're unable to offer the exact action or solution people are requesting, simply listening deeply, asking genuine questions, and extending care can go a long way. Often, if we listen closely enough, there is a small path forward that feels right to each of us.

In the weeks that followed my friend's conversation, the teacher went out of her way to check in about how her daughter was feeling about reading in class. This was above and beyond and demonstrated a true sense of care about her child's experience in the class.

There is power in the follow-up. When people follow up on details I've shared about my life or work, it makes me feel like they're truly interested in me and care about my well-being and success. This is not unique to relationships with adults. Following up with our students when they share with us is deeply impactful. I try to remember to do this. To be successful at it, we must live fully in the moment with others. I've heard others say that when our phones are visible on the table, it can pull us from the present moment. Even when our phones are facedown. This is why (most of the time) when I walk the building, I do so without my phone in my hand. It's in my pocket, and if there's an emergency, someone will call. Honestly, I'm happiest in these moments of my work. I am able to truly enjoy the incredible value that each staff member brings into our school community every day.

What we look for, we find. It's easy to overcomplicate things in education, but some of the most important moves we make are quite simple and impactful. The key is quieting the noise so we can stay close to what matters most. How we feel in the work impacts how others feel in the work, and all of this impacts how the work actually goes.

Thrill, delight, something special—whatever we want to call it—can mean very small moves we make on a daily basis, like the art of the follow-up, but it can also mean those bigger moments that only happen on occasion, all of which are valuable.

The Power of Play

Some of my most joyful memories include play. As adults, it's easy to underestimate the power of play. I believe that play is an essential part of a child's learning process, so recess is a vital element in every student's day. In their book *When You Wonder, You're Learning*, Gregg Behr and Ryan Rydzewski share enduring lessons from Mister Rogers. This quote about play is one I keep close: "'Play is often talked about as if it were a relief from serious learning,' Rogers once said. 'But for children, play *is* serious learning.'"[13] On the playground, children learn many lessons about playing fairly and taking care of others. Now, just because I believe recess is essential for all students doesn't mean I believe we don't teach behavior or intervene when we see unkind or unsafe behavior. Children will sometimes struggle to be kind with other children, and they'll need to be taught how to interact with others appropriately. Sometimes we can teach these lessons through participating in children's play ourselves. As an elementary principal, I joined countless games of kickball so I could be a participant and both model and support children in playing nicely and fairly. Footraces too. To this day, Jude Cantor, an elementary teacher, loves to talk about seeing a flash go by her classroom window and then seeing a slew of third-grade boys running behind me. It's important to wear sneakers because you just never know when you'll want to school some kids in a footrace at recess, ha! The truth is that I was having so much fun, and so were they, and that made us all feel more connected at school.

So many important life lessons are learned on the playground. Many of us understand this, but what can be difficult to see in the busyness of the workday is how important it is for us, as adults, to enjoy ourselves at work and to play alongside students. Some of my best work and my best thinking happens when I'm playful in my approach to the work. Play not only helps relieve stress, but it can unleash creative solutions and grow our relationships with each other.

As an elementary principal, I always found inside recess a bit stressful. Many kids benefit from running around outside, so it's disappointing when they don't have that opportunity. Sometimes, we would open the gym to give students a chance to run around and expend some energy. When the gym was not organized into zones, however, it could feel a little like that scene in *Kindergarten Cop* where kids are running around and Mr. Kimble has lost all control of the classroom. So, one afternoon I went into the gym to help out and have a little fun—because why not? If I was going to be working anyway, I may as well enjoy it.

Like I've said, I am a classically trained dancer. To this day, I love to dance. And on this particular day, I decided that I wanted to start a conga line at second-grade recess. So, I just started the conga by myself in the middle of the gymnasium. Balls whizzing by my head. Children chasing each other and screaming. It felt a bit brave to put myself in the middle of this chaos, but there we were. "Da-na-da-da-da-da . . . hey!" Some students stopped running. Others stopped their conversations. A young man placed his basketball on his hip, holding up the game. Kids started to giggle. A couple of students joined in. And then a few more. And before you knew it, I had most of the second grade behind me in a long conga line, everyone putting their own personal style and flair into it.

I can still remember the second-grade teachers laughing and taking pictures—a bit relieved that for even just a minute, recess felt organized. I'm not sure that I've ever seen second graders line up so fast. Perhaps if lining up to go inside felt more playful like a conga line, kids might be more inclined to put a little hustle in their steps. The conga felt more natural to me than a recess whistle to get their attention.

I had a great time with this. Students could tell I was really enjoying myself. They wanted to have fun too. While we are having fun, we are open to learning. It's really that simple. As Fred Rogers noted, "The best teacher in the world is the one who loves what he or she does, and just loves it in front of you."[14] The fun doesn't have to be limited to recess. In fact, the fun may be even more powerful in the classroom—though it's also important to remember that novelty is a key factor in fun. The principal was not found doing the conga on a daily basis. While we rightfully give a lot of attention to classroom routines and procedures and maintaining an orderly learning environment, our brains also benefit from unexpected moments of joy. As Chip and Dan Heath explain in *The Power of Moments*, "The reason we remember our youth so well is that it is a . . . time for firsts." They go on to explain, "Novelty changes our perception of time."[15] As Tania Luna and LeeAnn Renninger, PhD, the authors of the book *Surprise* say, "We feel most comfortable when things are certain, but we feel most alive when they're not."[16] This reminds me a bit of the random grouping strategy previously mentioned. There is an element of novelty when the teacher randomly selects the groups in front of the class. Beyond novelty for the sake of novelty, little moments of fun that shake up the expected routine have the power to improve our brain functions—specifically memory, as mentioned by Chip and Dan Heath above.

When searching for those special moments, the most important question to ask yourself is what sparks joy in you. How might you use that joy to thrill and delight others? I'm reminded of the Magic Castle Hotel near Disneyland. Chip and Dan Heath note that while the Magic Castle Hotel may not be much to look at, it's ranked among the top hotels in the LA area. It's not known for its sophistication or ambiance. No, it's known for creating experiences for guests. If you go to the pool, you'll find a cherry-red phone. You can pick up the receiver and someone will say, "Popsicle hotline" and take your order. Your popsicle is then delivered to you at the pool on a silver platter by someone wearing white gloves.[17] High class! What's your version of the popsicle hotline? We don't have to spend money on costumes or sweet treats. We just need to use our imaginations and consider that what gets us excited to come to work might also excite others. We need to keep dreaming up moments that can make school more engaging for all of us.

Physical Space

The way we organize our physical spaces also defines the moments we create and the way people feel when they spend time with us. If we're having a meeting with teachers and we sit at the head of a rectangular table, who's in charge? Whose meeting is this? The answer is clear. If we're seated at a round table, no one is solely in charge. This meeting belongs to all of us, and we all have equal say in this space. I love the magic of a round table. Peter Block describes the power of circles in *Community: The Structure of Belonging*: "Physical space is more decisive in creating community than we realize. Most meeting spaces are designed for control, negotiation, and persuasion. We always have a choice about the way we rearrange and occupy whatever room we are handed. Community is built when we sit in circles, when there are windows and the walls have signs of life, when every voice can be equally heard and amplified, when we all are on one level."[18] Certainly, larger circles feel different from smaller circles, and smaller circles tend to be more conducive to the exchange of ideas. In my experience, not every meeting room has windows or walls with signs of life, but the idea that I'm empowered to change the room configuration to best match the learning experience is an important and powerful one. The furniture or room does not need to be perfect for us to be positively impactful with the way we arrange it.

Meetings are a great place to model room configurations that foster desired learning outcomes. If our staff meetings, work sessions, or professional development are organized with teachers seated in rows facing the front of the room, we should not be surprised when this is how our classroom spaces are organized. Every move we make is modeling and sending a message about what we value. If our desks are in rows, we send the message that everyone's focus should be on the front of the room, and usually what can be found at the front of the room is the teacher. Sometimes, this is exactly where the focus needs to be, but if this is always where the focus is, we may be sending the message that the teacher's voice matters most in the classroom. It's difficult to build an engaging and connected learning community if there is one voice that matters most. Since school is hectic, people don't always pick up on the intentional modeling we do, which is why we need to not only model good practices for our students and staff but also name what we are doing and why we are doing it that way.

Molly Connaughton Teszlewicz, an educational consultant and former middle school principal, encourages teachers to use their room configurations to inspire happiness and interest in learning. It's so basic, but it makes a lot of sense because the first thing students see when they walk into our classrooms is how the desks and furniture are arranged. Christina Sherman, an educational consultant and former high school math teacher, recently shared that anytime her desks were in rows, her students would say, "Oh no! Do we have a test today?" I love that desks in rows were not the norm. Classroom configurations send messages about who has the power, whose voice matters, and what kind of student engagement is encouraged.

There is also research to support how critical proximity can be in nurturing trust and belonging. According to Daniel Coyle's book *The Culture Code*, one of the first people to formally attempt research on this was a young MIT professor named Thomas Allen. Upon studying the quality of work done by two engineering firms that were working on the same complex challenge, "Allen could find none [no factors] that played a meaningful role in cohesion. Except for one. The distance between their desks."[19] In short, when we spend time in close proximity to others, trust increases, and there is a high likelihood that the quality of our work improves too. Allen's research had further implications regarding the importance of eye contact and working on the same floor as those we collaborate with. This makes me wonder about the adults collaborating with each other in our schools. If we don't spend much time around each other, won't our ability to do high-quality work together be inhibited? Because if proximity builds trust, lack of proximity does not support trust. As far as classroom configuration conclusions, the following from Coyle is important: "In other words, proximity functions as a kind of connective drug. Get close, and our tendency to connect lights up."[20] It's important that we find opportunities to sit with our students and that they sit (and stand) with each other too. This means coming out from behind our teacher desks so there's not a constant barrier between us. I often find that when I converse with authority figures, I'm more connected and comfortable when they seat themselves at my table—and I'm even more connected and trusting when we're seated at a small round table together.

Imagine you're a student and you enter a classroom where the furniture configuration looks wildly different from previous days. Desks clustered all sorts of different ways. Or there's a note asking you to meet your teacher outside in the courtyard. Wow, a change of scenery! Finding temperate days to promote student learning outdoors can thrill and delight many students. As Ingrid Fetell Lee says in her book, *Joyful*, "In a study of elementary schools, students in classrooms with the most daylight advanced as much as 26 percent faster in reading and 26 percent in math over the course of a year."[21] So, if you don't have natural lighting in your classroom, you may advance learning when you take your students outside or into a different learning space that does offer natural lighting. Perhaps you're a secondary teacher, and you're overwhelmed considering how you might move the furniture in your room multiple times a day. If the students can do it, let them. Perhaps you could create a norm: when students enter the classroom, they look at the board to see what the configuration will be that day, and they set up the room before the bell rings. I've also heard of teachers using specific songs to indicate what the setup will be for the day. Before walking into the hallway to greet students, the teacher ensures that song is playing, and students begin setting up as they enter and hear the music.

A big part of our work as educators is making school a fun, enjoyable, and caring place for learners. When I say learners, I'm including us and our colleagues too. I was recently working with a high school teacher who was grappling with how to inspire students to learn math. We got to wondering what would make a student want to buy a ticket to come to class. Think about that. What would make staff and students want to run into our schools every day? Planning for that looks a bit different. What do we want students to learn, *and* what experience do we think they'll enjoy so much that they can't help but learn from it?

It all starts and ends with knowing the learners we serve. Michelle Dohrmann, a high school ELA teacher, is the professional who started the teacher academy in our high school. Michelle had a student who was continually, egregiously late to her English class. She was struggling to get this student to show up to class on time. So, Michelle decided to go eat lunch with this student at his table in the cafeteria and then join him for his walk to her class to ensure that he made it on time. This student seemed to really enjoy their lunch together. She joked with him during that walk back to her classroom. "Wow, see! You can do it! You can make it on time. We made it on time." After that lunch together, the student was rarely if ever late to her class. Michelle has been spotted enjoying lunch with small groups of students in the courtyard too. It's amazing what can happen when teachers take the time to connect with students as human beings. That deep, genuine sense of care can make a tremendous impact on students and their learning. When students experience a strong sense of care and belonging at school, meaningful learning is more accessible for them. When students feel like staff and peers would miss them if they were gone, they are more likely to come to school and go to class on time.

Noticing and caring about individuals is a brand worth having. People would buy a ticket to that. They would run toward it. I know I do.

Reflection Questions:

- How might you add a small element of thrill and delight to an upcoming meeting or lesson?

- What is something you loved when you were a kid? How might you bring some of that fun into the school environment?

- How might you incorporate elements of surprise into daily classroom or school routines to give learners, including yourself, a boost of happiness?

- How might you reconfigure your seating arrangements to support the way you want learners to feel? To support the learning?

CHAPTER 7

WHOLEHEARTED WORK

How do you change the world? One room at a time. Which room? The one you're in.

—PETER BLOCK

Much of this book is about leading ourselves first, modeling being a good human, and nurturing the conditions so others can do their best work. The way we think and talk about our work, the way we approach the work, the way we respond to people and problems—it can be contagious. Every interaction is an opportunity to grow the culture we desire for our schools and classrooms.

Every conversation and gathering is an opportunity to leave people and the work better than when we found it.

Schools are ecosystems, meaning they are living, breathing, interconnected organisms. Nothing happens in isolation, good or bad, so when we become deeply self-aware and committed to our own growth and development, it has a positive impact on everyone with whom we come into contact.

This is what makes schools such a special place. It's also what makes building a strong culture such a challenge because the work is never done. Learning is inherently social, and the more time we spend around each other, the more likely we will pick up on the habits and dispositions of the people with whom we spend the most time. This is why it's critical to know ourselves well and to understand the impact we are having on other people. If we show up to the staff lounge and complain about students and our work, the people sharing space with us are more likely to leave complaining about students and our work. Even if they don't leave with those behaviors, they leave feeling heavier, and their view of the work and students may be impacted.

We certainly need spaces and places where we can process hard things. It's the way we go about those conversations and the timing of those conversations that can support a healthy school culture. My husband works in college athletics. At games, it makes me cringe when fans yell rude comments about student athletes, especially when their parents are sitting just a few seats away. I try to remember that when I'm processing a situation and speaking about the people involved. Every person we serve is someone else's entire world. We can model what it means to process in a way that would sound constructive and productive if that person or their family was in the room with us. Sometimes, it's best to not say anything at all. Modeling no reaction or pausing is powerful. More people should press pause before firing up social media. Again, our kids are watching. The world is watching.

In earlier chapters, I talked about being strategic in deciding where we can do less so we can give more to what matters most. But I think for many of us, it feels like no amount of rest is enough. We are not rejuvenated after leaving work on time or a good night's sleep. No, this does not mean that we are lazy or unwilling to work hard. Continuing to feel worn down physically, mentally, and emotionally is a red flag that something isn't right.

We deserve to feel better—in part because we cannot give to others what we ourselves do not possess. David Whyte, author of *Crossing the Unknown Sea*, shares a conversation with a monk, Brother David, and there is a quote from Brother David that I often revisit: "You know the antidote to exhaustion is not necessarily rest? . . . The antidote to exhaustion is wholeheartedness."[1] Wholeheartedness accelerates meaningful learning. The *Merriam-Webster* dictionary describes wholehearted as "completely and sincerely devoted, determined, or enthusiastic" or "marked by complete earnest commitment" and "free from all reserve or hesitation."[2] In short, it feels like wholeheartedness is about showing up as our authentic selves with our full effort, energy, and care. While I've previously mentioned that not everything is worth this level of gusto, it is important that we do not lose our ability to show up this way. Being wholehearted makes us feel alive in our work and our purpose, and it fuels others with the energy to do the same. Marc Brackett, PhD, founding director of the Yale Center for Emotional Intelligence, states in his book, *Permission to Feel*, "Emotions are the most powerful force inside the workplace—as they are in every human endeavor."[3] There is no completely separating emotions from the work or from learning. Which means, much as we may try, we are not separate from our emotions or the emotions of others. The sooner we embrace this and see our internal work as part of the work of being an impactful educator, the sooner we can reach our biggest potential and can support others in doing the same.

According to Brené Brown's Wholehearted Living program, there are three areas that encompass wholeheartedness: love, belonging, and vulnerability.[4] When we are feeling the kind of exhaustion that this beautiful profession often brings, it's important to ask ourselves if perhaps one of these areas needs attention in our work. This chapter is not intended to be a full account of what it means to be wholehearted nor is it a thorough exploration of emotional intelligence. I'm no expert, and I continue to learn, unlearn, and relearn for myself. This chapter is merely the start of a very important conversation with yourself that will skim the surface of possibilities as you strive to understand how you're feeling in your work and how you can approach it more deeply. You are worthy, capable, and deserving of all that is good in this world. I invite you to gently make space for yourself and to kindly reflect on ways you would encourage someone you love.

Presence

It's inspiring when we meet people who say they love what they do. Especially when we can see that they genuinely mean it. I'm sure there will be people who read this book and think, "Seriously? Love? This job is so hard and now I need to love it and love everyone too?" So, I think it is critical to clarify the word *love* in the context of our work in education. What I notice about many people who say they love what they do is that they are fully present in the moment. They show up for themselves and others in ways that make people feel like what is most important is being with each other. Often, this kind of love, or presence, is more accessible when we are genuinely enjoying ourselves. Certainly, this looks different at work than it does at home, but it is valuable to have something we love in our work every day. Like water, we can only go for so long without it. Some days are going to be filled with more of what we don't love, and that's just part of the world of work. However, we can be mindful about how we feel and about how others are feeling and create little moments that truly fill us up and bring us joy. In earlier chapters, I mentioned creating moments of thrill and delight. Moments that make us all feel excited to come to school every day. However, if we are unable to be mindful and present in these moments, we miss them, and when we miss them, we miss the opportunity to embrace the positive emotions that accompany these moments. Have you ever been multitasking during a conversation and, upon hearing laughter, you realize you've missed out on the joke?

(Sometimes this is not a bad thing, ha!) Have you ever been sitting on the beach, enjoying the sun on your shoulders, scrolling through social media, and then all of a sudden someone seated next to you yells, "Look! A dolphin!" But by the time you look up, it's gone, and you've missed it? Yes, one of the most loving things we can do is give our full attention to others and to our shared experiences. This does wonders for those we serve and lead. However, it's equally if not more important for our own well-being. When we are present in the moment, there is more to notice, appreciate, and love about ourselves, others, and our shared experiences. Presence allows us to feel joy and connection instead of having to pretend we feel them, which can be tiring.

In her book *Evolving with Gratitude*, Lainie Rowell describes "savoring walks." In essence, you walk around your environment appreciating all the good that you may miss on a daily basis. Rowell explains, "We often think of savoring in the context of food and the ability to completely enjoy what we are eating or drinking. Savoring is really about the ability to enjoy anything fully. It is about being mindful of the experience and, more specifically, the internal or external stimuli that are responsible for the positive feelings we are experiencing. This is a twenty-minute practice that helps us tune into our sense of wonder to truly notice and appreciate the good around us."[5]

Savoring walks have the power to bring us into the present so we can appreciate what there is to love about that moment. Instructional coaches in my district call these praise walks. They travel throughout the building with teachers uncovering the great practices they find in other teacher's classrooms. They leave notes for those teachers, helping them to see with great specificity the impact they're having on student learning. These moments of appreciation from other practitioners are meaningful. Many teachers keep the notes they receive behind their desks as a reminder that they are appreciated for the small moves they make in the service of meaningful learning. But a savoring walk doesn't need to be a group event. When I'm feeling low on love in my work,

I can enjoy a good savoring walk even if it's a short stroll from one meeting to the next. I don't say to myself, "I'm going on a savoring walk today." I simply decide to put my phone away, walk around, and notice. Inevitably, there is something to love and appreciate. I find teachers taking great care of students and administrators taking good care of teachers. Often, when I'm walking around, I run into someone who generously reminds me of my impact and a small move I've made that they appreciate, and suddenly "Where is the love?" turns into "There is the love." Perhaps Ingrid Fetell Lee says it best in her book, *Joyful*: "Modern psychology likewise embraces this inward lens, suggesting that the way to a happy life is to change how we look at the world and our place in it."[6] When we look for the good in ourselves and others, we find it.

Sometimes, I think we shy away from this kind of presence because it opens us up to painful emotions as well. It means we will see, feel, and sit with others in their pain. It means we will be tuned into our own emotions like sadness, anger, or fear in a way that makes us feel like we cannot control whether we will cry or use a short tone with others. This is a reality. A friend of mine passed away recently, and I found myself weeping in my car as I headed into school to lead a special education supervisor's final evaluation meeting. Thankfully, my boss, Ellie Preston, who was also friends with this individual, invited me to take the time I needed, and if I needed to go home, I was free to do so. As I sat in my car, I was reminded of the show *Shrinking*, where Harrison Ford's character, a therapist named Dr. Paul Rhodes, encourages a high school student named Alice to set aside fifteen minutes each day to cry to sad songs to process her grief. When the fifteen minutes are up, it's time to try and go about her day.[7] This is portrayed in a somewhat comical manner like most of the content in the show, but it's comical because there is an underlying truth. The truth being that sometimes we don't allow ourselves to experience emotions because we're afraid of how long we will have to experience the discomfort of the emotions.

So, I turned on a song, and I cried my eyes out in my car. Then, I asked myself whether I would be able to truly focus on and celebrate this special education supervisor who was well deserving of glowing remarks. I decided I could do it and do it well, and that's what I did. If that had not been the case, that would have been OK too. I'm not saying that there aren't times to compartmentalize emotions. What I am saying is that if we always shut down our emotions, our experiences both good and bad become more muted. There is a bright, beautiful world out there for us to experience, alive with possibilities, and I don't want us to miss it.

Here are a few questions to support you in cultivating more presence in your work:

- When was the last time you felt excited about your work? The kind of excitement that makes the day go by quickly and causes you to lose yourself in the moment? What were the conditions that made that an enjoyable experience for you? How might you cultivate similar conditions for yourself and others?
- How might you incorporate a savoring walk into your daily or weekly work?
- When you find yourself multitasking or thinking about more than one thing, how might you kindly give yourself permission to set something aside so you can more fully experience the present moment? For example, when I'm reading or watching a show in the evening, I struggle with stressful work thoughts that creep into my mind. I keep a notebook by me so I can put those worries into a "later list." This way I know those worries are accounted for but I give myself the freedom to enjoy my downtime.

Belonging

Sometimes, our exhaustion doesn't come from not doing things we love at work, not being present with others, or not allowing ourselves to feel deeply. Sometimes, we feel that our voice doesn't matter to others, and this is the source of our exhaustion. Other times, we have a sense that the mission at hand is not the right mission. Or, a double hitter, we feel like we are on the wrong mission. So we use our voice to share our thoughts, but we don't get the sense that we are heard or that our concerns or ideas are taken into consideration.

I'm reminded of a critical moment. I was working on my principal's license and had just accepted a position as a middle school assistant principal. I was nervous and excited. After class, I shared my news with the professor and a few classmates who also lingered. I asked the professor what advice he had for me. Think about that for a moment. When we're nervous and excited, working on something interesting and relevant to us, working on something that feels big and challenging—so big, in fact, that we aren't sure we can pull it off—that's when our hearts and minds are most open to learning. So, I was ready to receive some really good advice from someone with experience and authority in that classroom. Without missing a beat, the professor said, "Wear pants." Huh. This man was giving me fashion advice? He was kidding, right? Even if he was kidding, I was so uncomfortable. Out of all the things that really matter in leadership, he was focused on pants? None of us said anything. I didn't respond and neither did my peers. This made me feel small. This made me want to be invisible. This was so far outside my leadership focus that I started to feel like maybe I didn't belong. It made me feel as if my leadership was some kind of joke to others.

Until it didn't. Because sometimes, the learning comes from what not to do. Yes, he was wrong, and I could go into all the reasons why that was wrong. But it was wrong that no one, including myself, spoke up about it. We were complicit in it. Often, when I struggle with belonging, it's not because I don't belong but because I struggle to belong to myself first. We cannot experience true belonging with others if we do not first belong to ourselves. We deserve to have our own back. And if our voice shakes or we can't speak up for ourselves and for what is right, we deserve to have others speak up. I belonged in that room and in conversations about leadership. Sadly, I'm not the only one who has experienced this. There are people all over the world in classrooms, schools, and workplaces who are made to feel like they don't belong. We must do our part to not only create belonging for ourselves but to create it for others. I'm reminded of these important words from Toni Morrison: "I tell my students, 'When you get these jobs that you have been so brilliantly trained for, just remember that your real job is that if you are free, you need to free somebody else. If you have some power, then your job is to empower somebody else.'"[8] We cannot center the humanity of others without this mindset. But we are human. All of us will make mistakes in the quest for our own belonging and in the quest to create belonging for others. It's how we respond to and learn from those mistakes that matters in the end. When we are wrong, we say we are wrong. When we have wronged someone in front of others, we let those who were there hear our apology too. Then, we learn from it and allow it to change our practices moving forward. My expectations for instruction and learning are high. My expectations for how we treat each other are even higher.

Here are a few questions to support you in cultivating belonging for yourself and others:

- When was the last time you had something hard to say and upon saying it, you had a sense that other people valued your perspective? What were the conditions that made that conversation feel safe?
- How might you nourish that same sense of safety and belonging for others?

- Who is someone you trust who can hold you accountable for the way others experience your authority in the classroom or school? How might you invite this person to share feedback with you in a manner that works best for you as a learner?

Vulnerability

Often, our exhaustion comes from feeling inauthentic. We are tired from acting the way we want to feel or acting the way we think other people expect us to act. There are likely good reasons for this. Perhaps others have perceived us negatively when we have shown up in authentic ways. Showing up in authentic ways requires vulnerability. To me, vulnerability means demonstrating that we don't have it all together and we don't have it all figured out. It is critical that we uncover what may be causing us to shy away from vulnerability and then determine how, where, and with whom we want to practice vulnerability. We all need spaces where we share our struggles and take healthy risks in our work. Vulnerability precedes trust. It does not follow it. Someone has to go first. It's critical we determine where we can go first or where someone else has first demonstrated vulnerability—and in turn, how we might extend trust and follow suit.

Let's explore risk-taking. Risk-taking requires vulnerability because when we take a risk, there's a chance our risk will lead to mistakes and that others will view those mistakes as a sign of weakness or being "less than" as a teacher. This has got to stop. I've heard administrators sound befuddled that they can't convince teachers to take risks and try new methods in their classrooms. I've heard teachers talk about how they can't get their students to take risks and try hard things. Are we modeling risk-taking and trying hard things in front of the people we serve? Are we talking about making mistakes, learning, and trying again? Or do we only talk about the things we've got figured out? If the standard we've set is that we always get things right on the first try, who's going to want to try something new?

If we don't practice learning from mistakes and we don't allow ourselves to be seen not knowing something, we've made our position seem exclusive. We've made being a teacher, instructional coach, or administrator something that only all-knowing people do. The truth is that none of us has it all figured out. We never will. That's the beauty of this complex educational landscape. We are constantly trying, learning, evolving, and leaning on each other. That's what more people need to see. They don't need to see shiny, perfect people.

As a writing teacher, I spent time in the summer with the Ohio Writing Project, working on my master's degree. I will never forget the opportunity to hear from a published author. He shared with us not only his book but all the messy drafts leading up to publication. It was incredibly powerful because for the first time ever, it dawned on me that authors don't just sit down and write their books perfectly from start to finish. I know it sounds wild that I would even think that—but when you can't see it, you don't know. When I saw that author's writing process, for the first time ever, I saw the possibility that I, too, could be an author.

I've been fortunate enough to stay connected with the Ohio Writing Project over the years, and I've appreciated not only those messy, honest moments from other writers but also the ways in which OWP has supported me in taking risks in my writing, classroom, and work. George Couros expands upon the need for modeling and support in his book *The Innovator's Mindset*: "If we want people to take risks, they have to know we are there to catch them and support them. They also need to see us leading by example and taking risks in our own work. Innovation is needed both in our classrooms and in our leadership. As leaders, we must model the kind of innovation we want to see."[9] Let's model and name the risks we are taking, why we are taking them, and what we learn when it doesn't go as planned. But beyond that, let's also support others when they try new things. Let's do everything in our power to remove obstacles to new ideas and practices that are good for students, staff, and their learning. Let's be thoughtful about how we respond to others when they make mistakes. Every conversation is an opportunity to make someone feel calm and capable in their learning.

When it comes to modeling vulnerability, if we want people to be more human in front of each other, if we want them to challenge themselves in the classroom, then we must show them what it looks like to be human, to struggle, and to learn from that struggle. Demystify it. Make it less intimidating and scary. I will never forget my conversation with a teacher who was talking about how it had been a really difficult school year. This twenty-year veteran teacher was thinking about moving away and starting over in another state to see if that might feel any different. The thought that we would lose an impactful teacher during a national shortage of educators hit my heart in a big way. I didn't have the answer. I didn't try to pretend I had the answer. And while I asked questions and listened for ways I might provide support, I was overcome by emotion thinking about how hard and impossible all of this felt. And I began to cry. The old rules of leadership would probably say that wasn't a good thing. We must be strong so our teachers know they can depend on us. We can't cry. We can't show that we don't know.

But modern leadership requires a different approach. It's not that we walk around all day with our hands in the air on the verge of tears. But we say when we don't know the answer, and we seek solutions together. When something is hard, we acknowledge that it's hard. And yes, sometimes we show emotion. In my case, sometimes I cry. Sometimes, I feel things in a big way because I have a lot of love to give to the people I serve.

Here are a few questions to support you in cultivating more vulnerability in your work:

- When was the last time you felt like your authentic self in your work? *Authentic* meaning you could feel that you weren't overthinking how others would perceive what was in your heart and mind.
- When was the last time you noticed someone else demonstrating vulnerability at work? What were the conditions that made that possible?
- How might you nourish the conditions needed to support vulnerability in yourself and others?
- What risk would you take in your work if you knew you couldn't fail? Do you believe deeply that a new idea or practice is good for learners? What is one small step you could take toward making it happen?

CONCLUSION

Sometimes the best way to feel better is counterintuitive. Sometimes I need to give that which I'm lacking. If I'm not experiencing connection with others, I make myself fully present. If I'm not feeling like I belong, I create belonging for others. And finally, someone has to be vulnerable and go first. Sometimes, that someone is me.

As Katie Martin says in *Learner-Centered Innovation*, "Teachers create what they experience."[1] Too often, we do not model the kinds of experiences we want for our students. If we want students to experience higher levels of happiness in our schools, we need to create experiences that promote the happiness of our staff. We spend a lot of time at work, so we may as well enjoy as much of it as possible. If we want adults to smile at kids and use their names, we must smile at the adults and use their names. If we want teachers to encourage students to interact with each other in the classroom, we must encourage adults to interact with each other at staff meetings, team meetings, and professional learning opportunities. If we want students to become deeply curious and involved in our classrooms, we need to create environments that foster deep curiosity and meaningful involvement for educators. If we want to promote critical thinking in our classrooms, we need to ensure that we aren't promoting a compliance-driven, permission-seeking culture with educators. You'll know you have a compliance-driven culture when you hear questions like these: "Is this what you wanted?" "Is this how you wanted me to do it?" "Did I write enough?" "Did I do enough?" Listen for that and instead of responding with a yes or no, see if it's appropriate to ask a question in return: "What do you think would be best here?" "Can you tell me more about that?" "And what else?"

If we want students to be deeply human and wholehearted in their learning, we need to show up that way ourselves.

Whether you achieve this through rest or more wholeheartedness yourself, I hope you find ways to be deeply human in the work you do. This is how you can inspire meaningful learning for others. Let's be educators who make others feel like they can expand beyond what they ever dreamed possible. Let's create space for learners—adults and students alike—to feel seen, known, understood, and appreciated. Let's make people feel that they are everything they should be while helping them grow into their greatest potential. It's the way you show up, treat others, and do the work that gives you real, long-lasting influence. Not your title.

My greatest inspiration comes from our students. Perhaps one student said it best: "I'm not sure that the perfect teacher exists, but the incredible teachers I've had aren't the ones who never make mistakes. They're the ones who never give up on me and have taught me that I should never give up on myself."

It's easy to overcomplicate our work in education, but some of the most important moves are quite simple and impactful. The key is quieting the noise so we can focus on what matters most. How we feel in the work impacts how others feel in the work, and both impact how the work actually goes.

Thank you for your commitment to nurturing the potential of other people's children and each other. Every time someone goes out into the world to do good, those who nurtured, inspired, and stretched them along the way are part of that person's story. Educators are changing the world through others every day. This is our legacy.

I know one thing for sure—it's how we show up for ourselves and each other that really matters in the end. What a beautiful opportunity we have to make a lasting impact on the world through small moves and moments with others. Let's treat others and these moments like they're special. Because they are. What I wouldn't give for one more conversation with my dad. One more song to sing at the top of our lungs in the car together. One more chance to hear him laugh and make others laugh too.

Greg Lawson was so very alive. He changed the world through his family and through me. I'm living this beautiful life for the both of us now, and I want my life to have meant something. I want to be someone who makes others feel alive and capable and inspired to make a positive difference.

Let's set the pressure of perfection, grand goals, and big gestures aside. Let's see the beauty in sunrises, smiles, kind words, and the people who simply show up every day. Let's hear it for the people who manage to keep their hearts open in world that can be harsh. A lot of those people are working in schools, and I think that's a beautiful legacy of learning.

NOTES

CHAPTER 1

1. Shawn Achor, "The Happy Secret to Better Work," filmed February 1, 2012, Bloomington, IN, TED video, 9:54 to 10:28, https://www.ted.com/talks/shawn_achor_the_happy_secret_to_better_work.
2. Achor, "The Happy Secret," 10:28 to 10:54.
3. J. B. Yeats, *J. B. Yeats Letters to His Son, W. B. Yeats, and Others, 1869–1922* (London: Faber and Faber), 1944, 121.
4. Rita Pierson, "Every Kid Needs a Champion," filmed April 2013 in New York, NY, TED video, 4:18 to 5:00, https://www.ted.com/talks/rita_pierson_every_kid_needs_a_champion.
5. Achor, "The Happy Secret," 10:31 to 10:39.
6. Dan Schawbel, "Shawn Achor: What You Need to Do before Experiencing Happiness," *Forbes*, September 10, 2013, https://www.forbes.com/sites/danschawbel/2013/09/10/shawn-achor-what-you-need-to-do-before-experiencing-happiness/.
7. JohnMark Taylor, "Mirror Neurons after a Quarter Century: New Light, New Cracks," Science in the News (blog), Harvard University, July 25, 2016, https://sitn.hms.harvard.edu/flash/2016/mirror-neurons-quarter-century-new-light-new-cracks/.
8. "How to Measure Employee Engagement with the Q12," Gallup, August 20, 2023, https://www.gallup.com/workplace/356045/q12-question-summary.aspx.
9. "7 Tools for Developing Teachers and Teaching," Rutherford Learning Group, http://www.rutherfordlg.com/new/wp/wp-content/uploads/2014/04/7toolsfordevelopingteachersandteaching.pdf.
10. "7 Tools," Rutherford, 2.
11. "Cognitive Behavior Therapy–StatPearls." 2023. NCBI. https://www.ncbi.nlm.nih.gov/books/NBK470241/

12 Laurel Mellin, *Wired for Joy: A Revolutionary Method for Creating Happiness from Within* (Carlsbad, CA: Hay House, 2010), 21.

CHAPTER 2

1 Jonathan Acuff, *Finish: Give Yourself the Gift of Done* (New York: Portfolio, 2017), 14–15.
2 George Couros and Katie Novak, *Innovate inside the Box: Empowering Learners through UDL and the Innovator's Mindset* (San Diego: Impress, 2019), 9.
3 John Spencer and A. J. Juliani, *Empower: What Happens When Students Own Their Learning* (San Diego: Impress, 2017), ix.

CHAPTER 3

1 Liz Forkin Bohannon, *Beginner's Pluck: Build Your Life of Purpose and Impact Now* (Grand Rapids, MI: Baker Books, 2019), 150.
2 Patrick Lencioni, *The Five Dysfunctions of a Team: A Leadership Fable* (San Francisco: Jossey-Bass, 2002), 106.
3 Thomas W. Many et al., *Energize Your Teams: Powerful Tools for Coaching Collaborative Teams in PLCS at Work* (Bloomington, IN: Solution Tree Press, 2021), 87–88.
4 Many et al., 87–88.
5 Henry Cloud, *Boundaries for Leaders: Results, Relationships, and Being Ridiculously in Charge* (New York: Harper Business, 2013), 13.
6 Brad Stulberg and Steve Magness, *Peak Performance: Elevate Your Game, Avoid Burnout, and Thrive with the New Science of Success* (Emmaus, PA: Rodale Books, 2017), 26.
7 Stulberg and Magness, *Peak Performance*, 79.

CHAPTER 4

1 Jonathan Acuff, *Finish: Give Yourself the Gift of Done* (New York: Portfolio, 2017), 17.

Notes

2 Acuff, 19.
3 James Clear, *Atomic Habits: An Easy & Proven Way to Build Good Habits & Break Bad Ones* (New York: Avery, 2018), 27.
4 Chris Field, *A Billion Hours of Good: Changing the World 14 Minutes at a Time* (Abilene, TX: Leafwood Publishers, 2021), 19.

CHAPTER 5

1 Shawn Achor, *Big Potential: How Transforming the Pursuit of Success Raises Our Achievement, Happiness, and Well-Being* (New York: Currency, 2018), 63.
2 Kristina Zeiser, "Study of Deeper Learning: Opportunities and Outcomes," American Institutes for Research, accessed April 23, 2023, https://www.air.org/project/study-deeper-learning-opportunities-and-outcomes.
3 Mag Gardner et al., "Engage Secondary Students Because the Future Depends on It," *New Pedagogies for Deep Learning: A Global Partnership, Deep Learning in Action Series*, no. 2 (May 2021): 3, https://deep-learning.global/wp-content/uploads/2021/05/Engage-Secondary-Students-Because-The-Future-Depends-on-it.pdf.
4 Rita Pierson: "Every Kid Needs a Champion." 2013. TED. https://www.ted.com/talks/rita_pierson_every_kid_needs_a_champion?language=en.
5 "TheStudentExperience21," Battelle for Kids, August 20, 2023, https://www.battelleforkids.org/how-we-help/the-student-experience21.
6 "The StudentExperience21."
7 Julia Freeland Fisher, "Not Just What but Who You Know Matters," *Education Next*, last updated August 29, 2018, https://www.educationnext.org/not-just-what-but-who-you-know-matters-freeland-fisher-excerpt/.

CHAPTER 6

1 Dwight L. Carter, *Be Great: Five Principles to Improve School Culture from the Inside Out* (San Diego: Impress, 2022), 156.
2 Will Guidara, *Unreasonable Hospitality: The Remarkable Power of Giving People More Than They Expect* (Toronto: Optimism Press, 2022), 182.
3 Terada, "Welcoming Students."
4 George Couros, *Because of a Teacher: Stories of the Past to Inspire the Future of Education* (San Diego: Impress, 2021), 36–37.
5 Adam Grant (@AdamMGrant), "We pay too much attention to the most confident voices—and too little attention to the most thoughtful ones," Twitter, December 9, 2022, 11:48 a.m., https://twitter.com/AdamMGrant/status/1601257372483059713.
6 Peter Liljedahl, *Building Thinking Classrooms in Mathematics, Grades K–12: 14 Teaching Practices for Enhancing Learning* (Thousand Oaks, CA: Corwin, 2020), 58–59.
7 Liljedahl, 46–47.
8 Liljedahl, 44–45.
9 Adam Grant (@AdamMGrant), "Time in meetings has more than tripled since Feb 2020. Nearly a third of meetings are unnecessary—wasting $25M a year for every 1k people," Twitter, September 30, 2022, 2:42 p.m., https://twitter.com/AdamMGrant/status/1575919115621249025.
10 Priya Parker, *The Art of Gathering: How We Meet and Why It Matters* (New York: Riverhead Books, 2018), 23.
11 Elena Aguilar, *The Art of Coaching Teams: Building Resilient Communities That Transform Schools* (San Francisco: Jossey-Bass, 2016), 170–171.
12 Aguilar, 171.
13 Gregg Behr and Ryan Rydzewski. *When You Wonder, You're Learning: Mister Rogers' Enduring Lessons for Raising Creative, Curious, Caring Kids.* (New York: Hachette Books, 2021), 64.

14 Behr and Rydzewski, 24–25.
15 Chip Heath and Dan Heath. 2017. *The Power of Moments: Why Certain Experiences Have Extraordinary Impact*. New York: Penguin Random House, 84–86.
16 Tania Luna and LeeAnn Renninger, PhD. *Surprise: Embrace the Unpredictable and Engineer the Unexpected* (New York: Penguin, 2015) xix–xx.
17 Heath, *The Power of Moments*, 9–11.
18 Peter Block, *Community: The Structure of Belonging* (Oakland, CA: Berrett-Koehler Publishers, 2018), 274.
19 Daniel Coyle, *The Culture Code: The Secrets of Highly Successful Groups* (New York: Bantam Books, 2018), 69.
20 Coyle, 70.
21 Ingrid Fetell Lee, *Joyful: The Surprising Power of Ordinary Things to Create Extraordinary Happiness* (New York: Little, Brown, 2018), 35.

CHAPTER 7

1 David Whyte, "Crossing the Unknown Sea (excerpt)," *Grateful Living*, accessed May 21, 2023, https://grateful.org/resource/crossing-unknown-sea/.
2 Merriam-Webster, s.v. "wholehearted (adj.)," August 20, 2023, http://www.merriam-webster.com/dictionary/wholehearted.
3 Marc Brackett, *Permission to Feel: Unlocking the Power of Emotions to Help Our Kids, Ourselves, and Our Society Thrive* (New York: Celadon Books, 2019), 219.
4 Hannah Aster, "Brené Brown. The 3 Aspects of Wholehearted Living," *Shortform*, August 1, 2021, https://www.shortform.com/blog/brene-brown-wholehearted-living/.
5 Lainie Rowell, *Evolving with Gratitude: Small Practices in Learning Communities That Make a Big Difference with Kids, Peers, and the World* (San Diego: Impress, 2022), 33.

6 Fetell Lee, *Joyful*, 3.
7 *Shrinking*, season 1, episode 3, "Fifteen Minutes," directed by Ry Russo-Young, written by Bill Lawrence, Jason Segel, and Brett Goldstein, featuring Jason Segel, Harrison Ford, and Jessica Williams, aired February 3, 2023, AppleTV+, Doozer Productions and Warner Bros. Television, 2023.
8 Pam Houston, "The Truest Eye," O, *The Oprah Magazine*, November 2003, 4.
9 George Couros, *The Innovator's Mindset: Empower Learning, Unleash Talent, and Lead a Culture of Creativity* (San Diego: Dave Burgess Consulting, 2015), 2.

Conclusion

1 Katie Martin, *Learner-Centered Innovation: Spark Curiosity, Ignite Passion and Unleash Genius* (San Diego: Impress, 2018), 233.

ACKNOWLEDGMENTS

I never thought I would write a blog, let alone a book. And then I met my good friend, George Couros. George encouraged me to write every week on a blog to reflect on my learning. I wrote my first blog post on September 10, 2020. Since then, I've written a blog post every week, and many of those reflections have inspired this book.

I would like to thank George Couros, who inspires me to become a better human being and educator. Not only through his work but through his belief in me and my greatest potential.

In this book, I wrote a lot about my dad, Greg Lawson, who taught me how to laugh and enjoy this precious life. I don't want to miss an opportunity to also thank my mom, Kim Lawson. She taught me how to be independent and strong in the face of adversity without allowing tough times to harden my heart. I'm beyond proud to be her daughter.

Thank you to my husband, Mario Mercurio, who has been incredibly gracious throughout this entire writing process. I promise to help with more house projects, like cleaning out the basement, upon the publication of this book.

Finally, thank you to Paige Couros and the editorial team for your support and encouragement. This isn't the book I started with but I think it's a better book because of all of you.

ABOUT MEGHAN LAWSON

Meghan is a thought leader who studies and implements the conditions and systems needed for transformational change. A lover of learning who believes in the goodness of people, Meghan works to cultivate spaces that honor the humanity of all people. She promotes storytelling, the exchange of ideas, and risk-taking. She is passionate about disrupting the status quo and creating kinder, forward-thinking communities of action. Meghan is also intensely curious about how to enhance the customer experience in schools. Meghan began her career in the English Language Arts classroom. So, inevitably, her mantra is "Words matter." She has worked in all levels of K–12 education as a teacher, school administrator, district administrator, and educational consultant.

MORE FROM IMPRESS

ImpressBooks.org

Empower
What Happens when Students Own Their Learning
by A.J. Juliani and John Spencer

Learner-Centered Innovation
Spark Curiosity, Ignite Passion, and Unleash Genius
by Katie Martin

Unleash Talent
Bringing Out the Best in Yourself and the Learners You Serve
by Kara Knollmeyer

Reclaiming Our Calling
Hold On to the Heart, Mind, and Hope of Education
by Brad Gustafson

Take the L.E.A.P.
Ignite a Culture of Innovation
by Elisabeth Bostwick

Drawn to Teach
An Illustrated Guide to Transforming Your Teaching
written by Josh Stumpenhorst and illustrated by Trevor Guthke

Math Recess
Playful Learning in an Age of Disruption
by Sunil Singh and Dr. Christopher Brownell

Innovate inside the Box
Empowering Learners Through UDL and Innovator's Mindset
by George Couros and Katie Novak

Personal & Authentic
Designing Learning Experiences That Last a Lifetime
by Thomas C. Murray

Learner-Centered Leadership
A Blueprint for Transformational Change in Learning Communities
by Devin Vodicka

Kids These Days
A Game Plan for (Re)Connecting with Those We Teach, Lead, & Love
by Dr. Jody Carrington

UDL and Blended Learning
Thriving in Flexible Learning Landscapes
by Katie Novak and Catlin Tucker

Teachers These Days
Stories & Strategies for Reconnection
by Dr. Jody Carrington and Laurie McIntosh

Because of a Teacher
Stories of the Past to Inspire the Future of Education
written and curated by George Couros

Because of a Teacher, Volume 2
Stories from the First Years of Teaching
written and curated by George Couros

Evolving Education
Shifting to a Learner-Centered Paradigm
by Katie Martin

Adaptable
How to Create an Adaptable Curriculum and Flexible Learning Experiences That Work in Any Environment
by A.J. Juliani

Lead from Where You Are
Building Intention, Connection, and Direction in Our Schools
by Joe Sanfelippo

The Shift to Student-Led
Reimagining Classroom Workflows with UDL and Blended Learning
by Catlin R. Tucker & Katie Novak

Evolving with Gratitude
Small Practices in Learning Communities That Make a Big Difference with Kids, Peers, and the World
by Lainie Rowell

The Design Thinking Classroom
Using Design Thinking to Reimagine the Role and Practice of Educators
by David Jakes

Be Great
Five Principles to Improve School Culture from the Inside Out
by Dwight Carter

Chasing Rabbits
A Curious Guide to a Lifetime of Mathematical Wellness
by Sunil Singh

Made in the USA
Las Vegas, NV
11 November 2023